Cratylus by Plato

Translated by Benjamin Jowett

INTRODUCTION

The Cratylus has always been a source of perplexity to the student of Plato. While in fancy and humour, and perfection of style and metaphysical originality, this dialogue may be ranked with the best of the Platonic writings, there has been an uncertainty about the motive of the piece, which interpreters have hitherto not succeeded in dispelling. We need not suppose that Plato used words in order to conceal his thoughts, or that he would have been unintelligible to an educated contemporary. In the Phaedrus and Euthydemus we also find a difficulty in determining the precise aim of the author. Plato wrote satires in the form of dialogues, and his meaning, like that of other satirical writers, has often slept in the ear of posterity. Two causes may be assigned for this obscurity: 1st, the subtlety and allusiveness of this species of composition; 2nd, the difficulty of reproducing a state of life and literature which has passed away. A satire is unmeaning unless we can place ourselves back among the persons and thoughts of the age in which it was written. Had the treatise of Antisthenes upon words, or the speculations of Cratylus, or some other Heracleitean of the fourth century B.C., on the nature of language been preserved to us; or if we had lived at the time, and been 'rich enough to attend the fifty-drachma course of Prodicus,' we should have understood Plato better, and many points which are now attributed to the extravagance of Socrates' humour would have been found, like the allusions of Aristophanes in the Clouds, to have gone home to the sophists and grammarians of the day.

For the age was very busy with philological speculation; and many questions were beginning to be asked about language which were parallel to other questions about justice, virtue, knowledge, and were illustrated in a similar manner by the analogy of the arts. Was there a correctness in words, and were they given by nature or convention? In the presocratic philosophy mankind had been striving to attain an expression of their ideas, and now they were beginning to ask themselves whether the expression might not be distinguished from the idea? They were also seeking to distinguish the parts of speech and to enquire into the relation of subject and predicate. Grammar and logic were moving about somewhere in the depths of the human soul, but they were not yet awakened into consciousness and had not found names for themselves, or terms by which they might be expressed. Of these beginnings of the study of language we know little, and there necessarily arises an obscurity when the surroundings of such a work as the Cratylus are taken away. Moreover, in this, as in most of the dialogues of Plato, allowance has to be made for the character of Socrates. For the theory of language can only be propounded by him in a manner which is consistent with his own profession of ignorance. Hence his ridicule of the new school of etymology is interspersed with many declarations 'that he knows nothing,' 'that he has learned from Euthyphro,' and the like. Even the truest things which he says are depreciated by himself. He professes to be guessing, but the guesses of Plato are better than all the other theories of the ancients respecting language put together.

The dialogue hardly derives any light from Plato's other writings, and still less from Scholiasts and Neoplatonist writers. Socrates must be interpreted from himself, and on first reading we certainly have a difficulty in understanding his drift, or his relation to the two other interlocutors in the dialogue. Does he agree with Cratylus or with Hermogenes, and is he serious in those fanciful etymologies, extending over more than half the dialogue, which he seems so greatly to relish? Or is he serious in part only; and can we separate his jest from his earnest?--Sunt bona, sunt quaedum mediocria, sunt mala plura. Most of them are ridiculously bad, and yet among them are found, as if by accident, principles of philology which are unsurpassed in any ancient writer, and even in advance of any philologer of the last century. May we suppose that Plato, like Lucian, has been amusing his fancy by writing a comedy in the form of a prose dialogue? And what is the final result of the enquiry? Is Plato an upholder of the conventional theory of language, which he acknowledges to be imperfect? or does he mean to imply that a perfect language can only be based on his own theory of ideas? Or if this latter explanation is refuted by his silence, then in what relation does his account of language stand to the rest of his philosophy? Or may we be so bold as to deny the connexion between them? (For the allusion to the ideas at the end of the dialogue is merely intended to show that we must not put words in the place of things or realities, which is a thesis strongly insisted on by Plato in many other passages)...These are some of the first thoughts which arise in the mind of the reader of the Cratylus. And the consideration of them may form a convenient introduction to the general subject of the dialogue.

We must not expect all the parts of a dialogue of Plato to tend equally to some clearly-defined end. His idea of literary art is not the absolute proportion of the whole, such as we appear to find in a Greek temple or statue; nor should his works be tried by any such standard. They have often the beauty of poetry, but they have also the freedom of conversation. 'Words are more plastic than wax' (Rep.), and may be moulded into any form. He wanders on from one topic to another, careless of the unity of his work, not fearing any 'judge, or spectator, who may recall him to the point' (Theat.), 'whither the argument blows we follow' (Rep.). To have determined beforehand, as in a modern didactic treatise, the nature and limits of the subject, would have been fatal to the spirit of enquiry or discovery, which is the soul of the dialogue...These remarks are applicable to nearly all the works of Plato, but to the Cratylus and Phaedrus more than any others. See Phaedrus, Introduction.

There is another aspect under which some of the dialogues of Plato may be more truly viewed:--they are dramatic sketches of an argument. We have found that in the Lysis, Charmides, Laches, Protagoras, Meno, we arrived at no conclusion--the different sides of the argument were personified in the different speakers; but the victory was not distinctly attributed to any of them, nor the truth wholly the property of any. And in the Cratylus we have no reason to assume that Socrates is either wholly right or wholly wrong, or that Plato, though he evidently inclines to him, had any other aim than that of personifying, in the characters of Hermogenes, Socrates, and Cratylus, the three theories of language which are respectively maintained by them.

The two subordinate persons of the dialogue, Hermogenes and Cratylus, are at the opposite poles of the argument. But after a while the disciple of the Sophist and the follower of Heracleitus are found to be not so far removed from one another as at first sight appeared; and both show an inclination to accept the third view which Socrates interposes between them. First, Hermogenes, the poor brother of the rich Callias, expounds the doctrine that names are conventional; like the names of slaves, they may be given and altered at pleasure. This is one of those principles which, whether applied to society or language, explains everything and nothing. For in all things there is an element of convention; but the admission of this does not help us to understand the rational ground or basis in human nature on which the convention proceeds. Socrates first of all intimates to Hermogenes that his view of language is only a part of a sophistical whole, and ultimately tends to abolish the distinction between truth and falsehood.

Hermogenes is very ready to throw aside the sophistical tenet, and listens with a sort of half admiration, half belief, to the speculations of Socrates.

Cratylus is of opinion that a name is either a true name or not a name at all. He is unable to conceive of degrees of imitation; a word is either the perfect expression of a thing, or a mere inarticulate sound (a fallacy which is still prevalent among theorizers about the origin of language). He is at once a philosopher and a sophist; for while wanting to rest language on an immutable basis, he would deny the possibility of falsehood. He is inclined to derive all truth from language, and in language he sees reflected the philosophy of Heracleitus. His views are not like those of Hermogenes, hastily taken up, but are said to be the result of mature consideration, although he is described as still a young man. With a tenacity characteristic of the Heracleitean philosophers, he clings to the doctrine of the flux. (Compare Theaet.) Of the real Cratylus we know nothing, except that he is recorded by Aristotle to have been the friend or teacher of Plato; nor have we any proof that he resembled the likeness of him in Plato any more than the Critias of Plato is like the real Critias, or the Euthyphro in this dialogue like the other Euthyphro, the diviner, in the dialogue which is called after him.

Between these two extremes, which have both of them a sophistical character, the view of Socrates is introduced, which is in a manner the union of the two. Language is conventional and also natural, and the true conventional-natural is the rational. It is a work not of chance, but of art; the dialectician is the artificer of words, and the legislator gives authority to them. They are the expressions or imitations in sound of things. In a sense, Cratylus is right in saying that things have by nature names; for nature is not opposed either to art or to law. But vocal imitation, like any other copy, may be imperfectly executed; and in this way an element of chance or convention enters in. There is much which is accidental or exceptional in language. Some words have had their original meaning so obscured, that they require to be helped out by convention. But still the true name is that which has a natural meaning. Thus nature, art, chance, all combine in the formation of language. And the three views respectively propounded by Hermogenes, Socrates, Cratylus, may be described as the conventional, the artificial or rational, and the natural. The view of Socrates is the meeting-point of the other two, just as conceptualism is the meeting-point of nominalism and realism.

We can hardly say that Plato was aware of the truth, that 'languages are not made, but grow.' But still, when he says that 'the legislator made language with the dialectician standing on his right hand,' we need not infer from this that he conceived words, like coins, to be issued from the mint of the State. The creator of laws and of social life is naturally regarded as the creator of language, according to Hellenic notions, and the philosopher is his natural advisor. We are not to suppose that the legislator is performing any extraordinary function; he is merely the Eponymus of the State, who prescribes rules for the dialectician and for all other artists. According to a truly Platonic mode of approaching the subject, language, like virtue in the Republic, is examined by the analogy of the arts. Words are works of art which may be equally made in different materials, and are well made when they have a meaning. Of the process which he thus describes, Plato had probably no very definite notion. But he means to express generally that language is the product of intelligence, and that languages belong to States and not to individuals.

A better conception of language could not have been formed in Plato's age, than that which he attributes to Socrates. Yet many persons have thought that the mind of Plato is more truly seen in the vague realism of Cratylus. This misconception has probably arisen from two causes: first, the desire to bring Plato's theory of language into accordance with the received doctrine of the Platonic ideas;

secondly, the impression created by Socrates himself, that he is not in earnest, and is only indulging the fancy of the hour.

1. We shall have occasion to show more at length, in the Introduction to future dialogues, that the so-called Platonic ideas are only a semi-mythical form, in which he attempts to realize abstractions, and that they are replaced in his later writings by a rational theory of psychology. (See introductions to the Meno and the Sophist.) And in the Cratylus he gives a general account of the nature and origin of language, in which Adam Smith, Rousseau, and other writers of the last century, would have substantially agreed. At the end of the dialogue, he speaks as in the Symposium and Republic of absolute beauty and good; but he never supposed that they were capable of being embodied in words. Of the names of the ideas, he would have said, as he says of the names of the Gods, that we know nothing. Even the realism of Cratylus is not based upon the ideas of Plato, but upon the flux of Heracleitus. Here, as in the Sophist and Politicus, Plato expressly draws attention to the want of agreement in words and things. Hence we are led to infer, that the view of Socrates is not the less Plato's own, because not based upon the ideas; 2nd, that Plato's theory of language is not inconsistent with the rest of his philosophy.

2. We do not deny that Socrates is partly in jest and partly in earnest. He is discoursing in a high-flown vein, which may be compared to the 'dithyrambics of the Phaedrus.' They are mysteries of which he is speaking, and he professes a kind of ludicrous fear of his imaginary wisdom. When he is arguing out of Homer, about the names of Hector's son, or when he describes himself as inspired or maddened by Euthyphro, with whom he has been sitting from the early dawn (compare Phaedrus and Lysias; Phaedr.) and expresses his intention of yielding to the illusion to-day, and to-morrow he will go to a priest and be purified, we easily see that his words are not to be taken seriously. In this part of the dialogue his dread of committing impiety, the pretended derivation of his wisdom from another, the extravagance of some of his etymologies, and, in general, the manner in which the fun, fast and furious, vires acquirit eundo, remind us strongly of the Phaedrus. The jest is a long one, extending over more than half the dialogue. But then, we remember that the Euthydemus is a still longer jest, in which the irony is preserved to the very end. There he is parodying the ingenious follies of early logic; in the Cratylus he is ridiculing the fancies of a new school of sophists and grammarians. The fallacies of the Euthydemus are still retained at the end of our logic books; and the etymologies of the Cratylus have also found their way into later writers. Some of these are not much worse than the conjectures of Hemsterhuis, and other critics of the last century; but this does not prove that they are serious. For Plato is in advance of his age in his conception of language, as much as he is in his conception of mythology. (Compare Phaedrus.)

When the fervour of his etymological enthusiasm has abated, Socrates ends, as he has begun, with a rational explanation of language. Still he preserves his 'know nothing' disguise, and himself declares his first notions about names to be reckless and ridiculous. Having explained compound words by resolving them into their original elements, he now proceeds to analyse simple words into the letters of which they are composed. The Socrates who 'knows nothing,' here passes into the teacher, the dialectician, the arranger of species. There is nothing in this part of the dialogue which is either weak or extravagant. Plato is a supporter of the Onomatopoetic theory of language; that is to say, he supposes words to be formed by the imitation of ideas in sounds; he also recognises the effect of time, the influence of foreign languages, the desire of euphony, to be formative principles; and he admits a certain element of chance. But he gives no imitation in all this that he is preparing the way for the construction of an ideal language. Or that he has any Eleatic speculation to oppose to the Heracleiteanism of Cratylus.

The theory of language which is propounded in the Cratylus is in accordance with the later phase of the philosophy of Plato, and would have been regarded by him as in the main true. The dialogue is also a satire on the philological fancies of the day. Socrates in pursuit of his vocation as a detector of false knowledge, lights by accident on the truth. He is guessing, he is dreaming; he has heard, as he says in the Phaedrus, from another: no one is more surprised than himself at his own discoveries. And yet some of his best remarks, as for example his view of the derivation of Greek words from other languages, or of the permutations of letters, or again, his observation that in speaking of the Gods we are only speaking of our names of them, occur among these flights of humour.

We can imagine a character having a profound insight into the nature of men and things, and yet hardly dwelling upon them seriously; blending inextricably sense and nonsense; sometimes enveloping in a blaze of jests the most serious matters, and then again allowing the truth to peer through; enjoying the flow of his own humour, and puzzling mankind by an ironical exaggeration of their absurdities. Such were Aristophanes and Rabelais; such, in a different style, were Sterne, Jean Paul, Hamann,--writers who sometimes become unintelligible through the extravagance of their fancies. Such is the character which Plato intends to depict in some of his dialogues as the Silenus Socrates; and through this medium we have to receive our theory of language.

There remains a difficulty which seems to demand a more exact answer: In what relation does the satirical or etymological portion of the dialogue stand to the serious? Granting all that can be said about the provoking irony of Socrates, about the parody of Euthyphro, or Prodicus, or Antisthenes, how does the long catalogue of etymologies furnish any answer to the question of Hermogenes, which is evidently the main thesis of the dialogue: What is the truth, or correctness, or principle of names?

After illustrating the nature of correctness by the analogy of the arts, and then, as in the Republic, ironically appealing to the authority of the Homeric poems, Socrates shows that the truth or correctness of names can only be ascertained by an appeal to etymology. The truth of names is to be found in the analysis of their elements. But why does he admit etymologies which are absurd, based on Heracleitean fancies, fourfold interpretations of words, impossible unions and separations of syllables and letters?

1. The answer to this difficulty has been already anticipated in part: Socrates is not a dogmatic teacher, and therefore he puts on this wild and fanciful disguise, in order that the truth may be permitted to appear: 2. as Benfey remarks, an erroneous example may illustrate a principle of language as well as a true one: 3. many of these etymologies, as, for example, that of dikaion, are indicated, by the manner in which Socrates speaks of them, to have been current in his own age: 4. the philosophy of language had not made such progress as would have justified Plato in propounding real derivations. Like his master Socrates, he saw through the hollowness of the incipient sciences of the day, and tries to move in a circle apart from them, laying down the conditions under which they are to be pursued, but, as in the Timaeus, cautious and tentative, when he is speaking of actual phenomena. To have made etymologies seriously, would have seemed to him like the interpretation of the myths in the Phaedrus, the task 'of a not very fortunate individual, who had a great deal of time on his hands.' The irony of Socrates places him above and beyond the errors of his contemporaries.

The Cratylus is full of humour and satirical touches: the inspiration which comes from Euthyphro, and his prancing steeds, the light admixture of quotations from Homer, and the spurious dialectic which is applied to them; the jest about the fifty-drachma course of Prodicus, which is declared on the best authority, viz. his own, to be a complete education in grammar and rhetoric; the double explanation of the name Hermogenes, either as 'not being in luck,' or 'being no speaker;' the dearly-bought wisdom of

Callias, the Lacedaemonian whose name was 'Rush,' and, above all, the pleasure which Socrates expresses in his own dangerous discoveries, which 'to-morrow he will purge away,' are truly humorous. While delivering a lecture on the philosophy of language, Socrates is also satirizing the endless fertility of the human mind in spinning arguments out of nothing, and employing the most trifling and fanciful analogies in support of a theory. Etymology in ancient as in modern times was a favourite recreation; and Socrates makes merry at the expense of the etymologists. The simplicity of Hermogenes, who is ready to believe anything that he is told, heightens the effect. Socrates in his genial and ironical mood hits right and left at his adversaries: Ouranos is so called apo tou oran ta ano, which, as some philosophers say, is the way to have a pure mind; the sophists are by a fanciful explanation converted into heroes; 'the givers of names were like some philosophers who fancy that the earth goes round because their heads are always going round.' There is a great deal of 'mischief' lurking in the following: 'I found myself in greater perplexity about justice than I was before I began to learn;' 'The rho in katoptron must be the addition of some one who cares nothing about truth, but thinks only of putting the mouth into shape;' 'Tales and falsehoods have generally to do with the Tragic and goatish life, and tragedy is the place of them.' Several philosophers and sophists are mentioned by name: first, Protagoras and Euthydemus are assailed; then the interpreters of Homer, oi palaioi Omerikoi (compare Arist. Met.) and the Orphic poets are alluded to by the way; then he discovers a hive of wisdom in the philosophy of Heracleitus;--the doctrine of the flux is contained in the word ousia (= osia the pushing principle), an anticipation of Anaxagoras is found in psuche and selene. Again, he ridicules the arbitrary methods of pulling out and putting in letters which were in vogue among the philologers of his time; or slightly scoffs at contemporary religious beliefs. Lastly, he is impatient of hearing from the half-converted Cratylus the doctrine that falsehood can neither be spoken, nor uttered, nor addressed; a piece of sophistry attributed to Gorgias, which reappears in the Sophist. And he proceeds to demolish, with no less delight than he had set up, the Heracleitean theory of language.

In the latter part of the dialogue Socrates becomes more serious, though he does not lay aside but rather aggravates his banter of the Heracleiteans, whom here, as in the Theaetetus, he delights to ridicule. What was the origin of this enmity we can hardly determine:--was it due to the natural dislike which may be supposed to exist between the 'patrons of the flux' and the 'friends of the ideas' (Soph.)? or is it to be attributed to the indignation which Plato felt at having wasted his time upon 'Cratylus and the doctrines of Heracleitus' in the days of his youth? Socrates, touching on some of the characteristic difficulties of early Greek philosophy, endeavours to show Cratylus that imitation may be partial or imperfect, that a knowledge of things is higher than a knowledge of names, and that there can be no knowledge if all things are in a state of transition. But Cratylus, who does not easily apprehend the argument from common sense, remains unconvinced, and on the whole inclines to his former opinion. Some profound philosophical remarks are scattered up and down, admitting of an application not only to language but to knowledge generally; such as the assertion that 'consistency is no test of truth:' or again, 'If we are over-precise about words, truth will say "too late" to us as to the belated traveller in Aegina.'

The place of the dialogue in the series cannot be determined with certainty. The style and subject, and the treatment of the character of Socrates, have a close resemblance to the earlier dialogues, especially to the Phaedrus and Euthydemus. The manner in which the ideas are spoken of at the end of the dialogue, also indicates a comparatively early date. The imaginative element is still in full vigour; the Socrates of the Cratylus is the Socrates of the Apology and Symposium, not yet Platonized; and he describes, as in the Theaetetus, the philosophy of Heracleitus by 'unsavoury' similes--he cannot believe that the world is like 'a leaky vessel,' or 'a man who has a running at the nose'; he attributes the flux of the world to the swimming in some folks' heads. On the other hand, the relation of thought to language is omitted here, but is treated of in the Sophist. These grounds are not sufficient to enable us to arrive at a precise conclusion. But we shall not be far wrong in placing the Cratylus about the middle, or at any rate in the first half, of the series.

Cratylus, the Heracleitean philosopher, and Hermogenes, the brother of Callias, have been arguing about names; the former maintaining that they are natural, the latter that they are conventional. Cratylus affirms that his own is a true name, but will not allow that the name of Hermogenes is equally true. Hermogenes asks Socrates to explain to him what Cratylus means; or, far rather, he would like to know, What Socrates himself thinks about the truth or correctness of names? Socrates replies, that hard is knowledge, and the nature of names is a considerable part of knowledge: he has never been to hear the fifty-drachma course of Prodicus; and having only attended the single-drachma course, he is not competent to give an opinion on such matters. When Cratylus denies that Hermogenes is a true name, he supposes him to mean that he is not a true son of Hermes, because he is never in luck. But he would like to have an open council and to hear both sides.

Hermogenes is of opinion that there is no principle in names; they may be changed, as we change the names of slaves, whenever we please, and the altered name is as good as the original one.

You mean to say, for instance, rejoins Socrates, that if I agree to call a man a horse, then a man will be rightly called a horse by me, and a man by the rest of the world? But, surely, there is in words a true and a false, as there are true and false propositions. If a whole proposition be true or false, then the parts of a proposition may be true or false, and the least parts as well as the greatest; and the least parts are names, and therefore names may be true or false. Would Hermogenes maintain that anybody may give a name to anything, and as many names as he pleases; and would all these names be always true at the time of giving them? Hermogenes replies that this is the only way in which he can conceive that names are correct; and he appeals to the practice of different nations, and of the different Hellenic tribes, in confirmation of his view. Socrates asks, whether the things differ as the words which represent them differ:--Are we to maintain with Protagoras, that what appears is? Hermogenes has always been puzzled about this, but acknowledges, when he is pressed by Socrates, that there are a few very good men in the world, and a great many very bad; and the very good are the wise, and the very bad are the foolish; and this is not mere appearance but reality. Nor is he disposed to say with Euthydemus, that all things equally and always belong to all men; in that case, again, there would be no distinction between bad and good men. But then, the only remaining possibility is, that all things have their several distinct natures, and are independent of our notions about them. And not only things, but actions, have distinct natures, and are done by different processes. There is a natural way of cutting or burning, and a natural instrument with which men cut or burn, and any other way will fail;--this is true of all actions. And speaking is a kind of action, and naming is a kind of speaking, and we must name according to a natural process, and with a proper instrument. We cut with a knife, we pierce with an awl, we weave with a shuttle, we name with a name. And as a shuttle separates the warp from the woof, so a name distinguishes the natures of things. The weaver will use the shuttle well,--that is, like a weaver; and the teacher will use the name well,--that is, like a teacher. The shuttle will be made by the carpenter; the awl by the smith or skilled person. But who makes a name? Does not the law give names, and does not the teacher receive them from the legislator? He is the skilled person who makes them, and of all skilled workmen he is the rarest. But how does the carpenter make or repair the shuttle, and to what will he look? Will he not look at the ideal which he has in his mind? And as the different kinds of work differ, so ought the instruments which make them to differ. The several kinds of shuttles ought to answer in material and form to the several kinds of webs. And the legislator ought to know the different materials and forms of which names are made in Hellas and other countries. But who is to be the judge of the proper form? The judge of shuttles is the weaver who uses them; the judge of lyres is the player of the lyre; the judge of ships is the pilot. And will not the judge who is able to direct the legislator in his work of naming, be he who knows how to use the names--he who can ask and answer questions--in short, the dialectician? The pilot directs the carpenter how to make the rudder, and the dialectician directs the legislator how he is to impose names; for to express the ideal forms of things in syllables and letters is not the easy task, Hermogenes, which you imagine.

'I should be more readily persuaded, if you would show me this natural correctness of names.'

Indeed I cannot; but I see that you have advanced; for you now admit that there is a correctness of names, and that not every one can give a name. But what is the nature of this correctness or truth, you must learn from the Sophists, of whom your brother Callias has bought his reputation for wisdom rather dearly; and since they require to be paid, you, having no money, had better learn from him at second-hand. 'Well, but I have just given up Protagoras, and I should be inconsistent in going to learn of him.' Then if you reject him you may learn of the poets, and in particular of Homer, who distinguishes the names given by Gods and men to the same things, as in the verse about the river God who fought with Hephaestus, 'whom the Gods call Xanthus, and men call Scamander;' or in the lines in which he mentions the bird which the Gods call 'Chalcis,' and men 'Cymindis;' or the hill which men call 'Batieia,' and the Gods 'Myrinna's Tomb.' Here is an important lesson; for the Gods must of course be right in their use of names. And this is not the only truth about philology which may be learnt from Homer. Does he not say that Hector's son had two names--

'Hector called him Scamandrius, but the others Astyanax'?

Now, if the men called him Astyanax, is it not probable that the other name was conferred by the women? And which are more likely to be right--the wiser or the less wise, the men or the women? Homer evidently agreed with the men: and of the name given by them he offers an explanation;--the boy was called Astyanax ('king of the city'), because his father saved the city. The names Astyanax and Hector, moreover, are really the same,--the one means a king, and the other is 'a holder or possessor.' For as the lion's whelp may be called a lion, or the horse's foal a foal, so the son of a king may be called a king. But if the horse had produced a calf, then that would be called a calf. Whether the syllables of a name are the same or not makes no difference, provided the meaning is retained. For example; the names of letters, whether vowels or consonants, do not correspond to their sounds, with the exception of epsilon, upsilon, omicron, omega. The name Beta has three letters added to the sound--and yet this does not alter the sense of the word, or prevent the whole name having the value which the legislator intended. And the same may be said of a king and the son of a king, who like other animals resemble each other in the course of nature; the words by which they are signified may be disguised, and yet amid differences of sound the etymologist may recognise the same notion, just as the physician recognises the power of the same drugs under different disguises of colour and smell. Hector and Astyanax have only one letter alike, but they have the same meaning; and Agis (leader) is altogether different in sound from Polemarchus (chief in war), or Eupolemus (good warrior); but the two words present the same idea of leader or general, like the words Iatrocles and Acesimbrotus, which equally denote a physician. The son succeeds the father as the foal succeeds the horse, but when, out of the course of nature, a prodigy occurs, and the offspring no longer resembles the parent, then the names no longer agree. This may be illustrated by the case of Agamemnon and his son Orestes, of whom the former has a name significant of his patience at the siege of Troy; while the name of the latter indicates his savage, man-of-the-mountain nature. Atreus again, for his murder of Chrysippus, and his cruelty to Thyestes, is rightly named Atreus, which, to the eye of the etymologist, is ateros (destructive), ateires (stubborn), atreotos (fearless); and Pelops is o ta pelas oron (he who sees what is near only), because in his eagerness to win Hippodamia, he was unconscious of the remoter consequences which the murder of Myrtilus would entail upon his race. The name Tantalus, if slightly changed, offers two etymologies; either apo tes tou lithou talanteias, or apo tou talantaton einai, signifying at once the hanging of the stone over his head in the world below, and the misery which he brought upon his country. And the name of his father, Zeus, Dios, Zenos, has an excellent meaning, though hard to be understood, because really a sentence which is divided into two parts (Zeus, Dios). For he, being the lord and king of all, is the author of our being, and in him all live: this is implied in the double form, Dios, Zenos, which being put together and interpreted is di on ze panta. There may, at first sight, appear to be some irreverence in calling him the son of Cronos, who is a proverb for stupidity; but the meaning is that Zeus himself is the son of a mighty intellect; Kronos, quasi koros, not in the sense of a youth, but quasi to katharon kai akeraton tou nou--the pure and garnished mind, which in turn is begotten of Uranus, who is so called apo tou oran ta ano, from looking upwards; which, as philosophers say, is the way to have a pure mind. The earlier portion of Hesiod's genealogy has escaped my memory, or I would try more conclusions of the same sort. 'You talk like an oracle.' I caught the infection from Euthyphro, who gave me a long lecture which began at dawn, and has not only entered into my ears, but filled my soul, and my intention is to yield to the inspiration to-day; and to-morrow I will be exorcised by some priest or sophist. 'Go on; I am anxious to hear the rest.' Now that we have a general notion, how shall we proceed? What names will afford the most crucial test of natural fitness? Those of heroes and ordinary men are often deceptive, because they are patronymics or expressions of a wish; let us try gods and demi-gods. Gods are so called, apo tou thein, from the verb 'to run;' because the sun, moon, and stars run about the heaven; and they being the original gods of the Hellenes, as they still are of the Barbarians, their name is given to all Gods. The demons are the golden race of Hesiod, and by golden he means not literally golden, but good; and they are called demons, quasi daemones, which in old Attic was used for daimones--good men are well said to become daimones when they die, because they are knowing. Eros (with an epsilon) is the same word as eros (with an eta): 'the sons of God saw the daughters of men that they were fair;' or perhaps they were a species of sophists or rhetoricians, and so called apo tou erotan, or eirein, from their habit of spinning questions; for eirein is equivalent to legein. I get all this from Euthyphro; and now a new and ingenious idea comes into my mind, and, if I am not careful, I shall be wiser than I ought to be by to-morrow's dawn. My idea is, that we may put in and pull out letters at pleasure and alter the accents (as, for example, Dii philos may be turned into Diphilos), and we may make words into sentences and sentences into words. The name anthrotos is a case in point, for a letter has been omitted and the accent changed; the original meaning being o anathron a opopen--he who looks up at what he sees. Psuche may be thought to be the reviving, or refreshing, or animating principle--e anapsuchousa to soma; but I am afraid that Euthyphro and his disciples will scorn this derivation, and I must find another: shall we identify the soul with the 'ordering mind' of Anaxagoras, and say that psuche, quasi phuseche = e phusin echei or ochei?--this might easily be refined into psyche. 'That is a more artistic etymology.'

After psuche follows soma; this, by a slight permutation, may be either = (1) the 'grave' of the soul, or (2) may mean 'that by which the soul signifies (semainei) her wishes.' But more probably, the word is Orphic, and simply denotes that the body is the place of ward in which the soul suffers the penalty of sin,--en o sozetai. 'I should like to hear some more explanations of the names of the Gods, like that excellent one of Zeus.' The truest names of the Gods are those which they give themselves; but these are unknown to us. Less true are those by which we propitiate them, as men say in prayers, 'May he graciously receive any name by which I call him.' And to avoid offence, I should like to let them know beforehand that we are not presuming to enquire about them, but only about the names which they usually bear. Let us begin with Hestia. What did he mean who gave the name Hestia? 'That is a very difficult question.' O, my dear Hermogenes, I believe that there was a power of philosophy and talk among the first inventors of names, both in our own and in other languages; for even in foreign words a principle is discernible. Hestia is the same with esia, which is an old form of ousia, and means the first principle of things: this agrees with the fact that to Hestia the first sacrifices are offered. There is also another reading--osia, which implies that 'pushing' (othoun) is the first principle of all things. And here I seem to discover a delicate allusion to the flux of Heracleitus--that antediluvian philosopher who cannot walk twice in the same stream; and this flux of his may accomplish yet greater marvels. For the names Cronos and Rhea cannot have been accidental; the giver of them must have known something about the doctrine of Heracleitus. Moreover, there is a remarkable coincidence in the words of Hesiod, when he speaks of Oceanus, 'the origin of Gods;' and in the verse of Orpheus, in which he describes Oceanus espousing his sister Tethys. Tethys is nothing more than the name of a spring--to diattomenon kai ethoumenon. Poseidon is posidesmos, the chain of the feet, because you cannot walk on the sea--the epsilon is inserted by way of ornament; or perhaps the name may have been originally polleidon, meaning, that the God knew many things (polla eidos): he may also be the shaker, apo tou seiein,--in this case, pi and delta have been added. Pluto is connected with ploutos, because wealth comes out of the earth; or the word may be a euphemism for Hades, which is usually derived apo tou aeidous, because the God is concerned with the invisible. But the name Hades was really given him from his knowing (eidenai) all good things. Men in general are foolishly afraid of him, and talk with horror of the world below from which no one may return. The reason why his subjects never wish to come back, even if they could, is that the God enchains them by the strongest of spells, namely by the desire of virtue, which they hope to obtain by constant association with him. He is the perfect and accomplished Sophist and the great benefactor of the other world; for he has much more than he wants there, and hence he is called Pluto or the rich. He will have nothing to do with the souls of men while in the body, because he cannot work his will with them so long as they are confused and entangled by fleshly lusts. Demeter is the mother and giver of food--e didousa meter tes edodes. Here is erate tis, or perhaps the legislator may have been thinking of the weather, and has merely transposed the letters of the word aer. Pherephatta, that word of awe, is pheretapha, which is only an euphonious contraction of e tou pheromenou ephaptomene,--all things are in motion, and she in her wisdom moves with them, and the wise God Hades consorts with her--there is nothing very terrible in this, any more than in the her other appellation Persephone, which is also significant of her wisdom (sophe). Apollo is another name, which is supposed to have some dreadful meaning, but is susceptible of at least four perfectly innocent explanations. First, he is the purifier or purger or absolver (apolouon); secondly, he is the true diviner, Aplos, as he is called in the Thessalian dialect (aplos = aplous, sincere); thirdly, he is the archer (aei ballon), always shooting; or again, supposing alpha to mean ama or omou, Apollo becomes equivalent to ama polon, which points to both his musical and his heavenly attributes; for there is a 'moving together' alike in music and in the harmony of the spheres. The second lambda is inserted in order to avoid the ill-omened sound of destruction. The Muses are so called--apo tou mosthai. The gentle Leto or Letho is named from her willingness (ethelemon), or because she is ready to forgive and forget (lethe). Artemis is so called from her healthy well-balanced nature, dia to artemes, or as aretes istor; or as a lover of virginity, aroton misesasa. One of these explanations is probably true,--perhaps all of them. Dionysus is o didous ton oinon, and oinos is quasi oionous because wine makes those think (oiesthai) that they have a mind (nous) who have none. The established derivation of Aphrodite dia ten tou athrou genesin may be accepted on the authority of Hesiod. Again, there is the name of Pallas, or Athene, which we, who are Athenians, must not forget. Pallas is derived from armed dances--apo tou pallein ta opla. For Athene we must turn to the allegorical interpreters of Homer, who make the name equivalent to theonoe, or possibly the word was originally ethonoe and signified moral intelligence (en ethei noesis). Hephaestus, again, is the lord of light--o tou phaeos istor. This is a good notion; and, to prevent any other getting into our heads, let us go on to Ares. He is the manly one (arren), or the unchangeable one (arratos). Enough of the Gods; for, by the Gods, I am afraid of them; but if you suggest other words, you will see how the horses of Euthyphro prance. 'Only one more God; tell me about my godfather Hermes.' He is ermeneus, the messenger or cheater or thief or bargainer; or o eirein momenos, that is, eiremes or ermes--the speaker or contriver of speeches. 'Well said Cratylus, then, that I am no son of Hermes.' Pan, as the son of Hermes, is speech or the brother of speech, and is called Pan because speech indicates everything--o pan menuon. He has two forms, a true and a false; and is in the upper part smooth, and in the lower part shaggy. He is the goat of Tragedy, in which there are plenty of falsehoods.

'Will you go on to the elements--sun, moon, stars, earth, aether, air, fire, water, seasons, years?' Very good: and which shall I take first? Let us begin with elios, or the sun. The Doric form elios helps us to see that he is so called because at his rising he gathers (alizei) men together, or because he rolls about (eilei) the earth, or because he variegates (aiolei = poikillei) the earth. Selene is an anticipation of Anaxagoras, being a contraction of selaenoneoaeia, the light (selas) which is ever old and new, and which, as Anaxagoras says, is borrowed from the sun; the name was harmonized into selanaia, a form which is still in use. 'That is a true dithyrambic name.' Meis is so called apo tou meiousthai, from suffering diminution, and astron is from astrape (lightning), which is an improvement of anastrope, that which turns the eyes inside out. 'How do you explain pur n udor?' I suspect that pur, which, like udor n kuon, is found in Phrygian, is a foreign word; for the Hellenes have borrowed much from the barbarians, and I always resort to this theory of a foreign origin when I am at a loss. Aer may be explained, oti airei ta apo tes ges; or, oti aei rei; or, oti pneuma ex autou ginetai (compare the poetic word aetai). So aither quasi aeitheer oti aei thei peri ton aera: ge, gaia quasi genneteira (compare the Homeric form gegaasi); ora (with an omega), or, according to the old Attic form ora (with an omicron), is derived apo tou orizein, because it divides the year; eniautos and etos are the same thought--o en eauto etazon, cut into two parts, en eauto and etazon, like di on ze into Dios and Zenos.

'You make surprising progress.' True; I am run away with, and am not even yet at my utmost speed. 'I should like very much to hear your account of the virtues. What principle of correctness is there in those charming words, wisdom, understanding, justice, and the rest?' To explain all that will be a serious business; still, as I have put on the lion's skin, appearances must be maintained. My opinion is, that primitive men were like some modern philosophers, who, by always going round in their search after the nature of things, become dizzy; and this phenomenon, which was really in themselves, they imagined to take place in the external world. You have no doubt remarked, that the doctrine of the universal flux, or generation of things, is indicated in names. 'No, I never did.' Phronesis is only phoras kai rou noesis, or perhaps phoras onesis, and in any case is connected with pheresthai; gnome is gones skepsis kai nomesis; noesis is neou or gignomenon esis; the word neos implies that creation is always going on--the original form was neoesis; sophrosune is soteria phroneseos; episteme is e epomene tois pragmasin--the faculty which keeps close, neither anticipating nor lagging behind; sunesis is equivalent to sunienai, sumporeuesthai ten psuche, and is a kind of conclusion--sullogismos tis, akin therefore in idea to episteme; sophia is very difficult, and has a foreign look--the meaning is, touching the motion or stream of things, and may be illustrated by the poetical esuthe and the Lacedaemonian proper name Sous, or Rush; agathon is ro agaston en te tachuteti,--for all things are in motion, and some are swifter than others: dikaiosune is clearly e tou dikaiou sunesis. The word dikaion is more troublesome, and appears to mean the subtle penetrating power which, as the lovers of motion say, preserves all things, and is the cause of all things, quasi diaion going through--the letter kappa being inserted for the sake of euphony. This is a great mystery which has been confided to me; but when I ask for an explanation I am thought obtrusive, and another derivation is proposed to me. Justice is said to be o kaion, or the sun; and when I joyfully repeat this beautiful notion, I am answered, 'What, is there no justice when the sun is down?' And when I entreat my questioner to tell me his own opinion, he replies, that justice is fire in the abstract, or heat in the abstract; which is not very intelligible. Others laugh at such notions, and say with Anaxagoras, that justice is the ordering mind. 'I think that some one must have told you this.' And not the rest? Let me proceed then, in the hope of proving to you my originality. Andreia is quasi anpeia quasi e ano roe, the stream which flows upwards, and is opposed to injustice, which clearly hinders the principle of penetration; arren and aner have a similar derivation; gune is the same as gone; thelu is derived apo tes theles, because the teat makes things flourish (tethelenai), and the word thallein itself implies increase of youth, which is swift and sudden ever (thein and allesthai). I am getting over the ground fast: but much has still to be explained. There is techne, for instance. This, by an aphaeresis of tau and an epenthesis of omicron in two places, may be identified with echonoe, and signifies 'that which has mind.'

'A very poor etymology.' Yes; but you must remember that all language is in process of change; letters are taken in and put out for the sake of euphony, and time is also a great alterer of words. For example, what business has the letter rho in the word katoptron, or the letter sigma in the word sphigx? The additions are often such that it is impossible to make out the original word; and yet, if you may put in and pull out, as you like, any name is equally good for any object. The fact is, that great dictators of literature like yourself should observe the rules of moderation. 'I will do my best.' But do not be too much of a precisian, or you will paralyze me. If you will let me add mechane, apo tou mekous, which means polu, and anein, I shall be at the summit of my powers, from which elevation I will examine the two words kakia and arete. The first is easily explained in accordance with what has preceded; for all things being in a flux, kakia is to kakos ion. This derivation is illustrated by the word deilia, which ought to have come after andreia, and may be regarded as o lian desmos tes psuches, just as aporia signifies an impediment to motion (from alpha not, and poreuesthai to go), and arete is euporia, which is the opposite of this--the everflowing (aei reousa or aeireite), or the eligible, quasi airete. You will think that I am inventing, but I say that if kakia is right, then arete is also right. But what is kakon? That is a very obscure word, to which I can only apply my old notion and declare that kakon is a foreign word. Next, let us proceed to kalon, aischron. The latter is doubtless contracted from aeischoroun, quasi aei ischon roun. The inventor of words being a patron of the flux, was a great enemy to stagnation. Kalon is to kaloun ta pragmata--this is mind (nous or dianoia); which is also the principle of beauty; and which doing the works of beauty, is therefore rightly called the beautiful. The meaning of sumpheron is explained by previous examples;--like episteme, signifying that the soul moves in harmony with the world (sumphora, sumpheronta). Kerdos is to pasi kerannumenon--that which mingles with all things: lusiteloun is equivalent to to tes phoras luon to telos, and is not to be taken in the vulgar sense of gainful, but rather in that of swift, being the principle which makes motion immortal and unceasing; ophelimon is apo tou ophellein--that which gives increase: this word, which is Homeric, is of foreign origin. Blaberon is to blamton or boulomenon aptein tou rou--that which injures or seeks to bind the stream. The proper word would be boulapteroun, but this is too much of a mouthful--like a prelude on the flute in honour of Athene. The word zemiodes is difficult; great changes, as I was saying, have been made in words, and even a small change will alter their meaning very much. The word deon is one of these disguised words. You know that according to the old pronunciation, which is especially affected by the women, who are great conservatives, iota and delta were used where we should now use eta and zeta: for example, what we now call emera was formerly called imera; and this shows the meaning of the word to have been 'the desired one coming after night,' and not, as is often supposed, 'that which makes things gentle' (emera). So again, zugon is duogon, quasi desis duein eis agogen--(the binding of two together for the purpose of drawing.) Deon, as ordinarily written, has an evil sense, signifying the chain (desmos) or hindrance of motion; but in its ancient form dion is expressive of good, quasi diion, that which penetrates or goes through all. Zemiodes is really demiodes, and means that which binds motion (dounti to ion): edone is e pros ten onrsin teinousa praxis--the delta is an insertion: lupe is derived apo tes dialuseos tou somatos: ania is from alpha and ienai, to go: algedon is a foreign word, and is so called apo tou algeinou: odune is apo tes enduseos tes lupes: achthedon is in its very sound a burden: chapa expresses the flow of soul: terpsis is apo tou terpnou, and terpnon is properly erpnon, because the sensation of pleasure is likened to a breath (pnoe) which creeps (erpei) through the soul: euphrosune is named from pheresthai, because the soul moves in harmony with nature: epithumia is e epi ton thumon iousa dunamis: thumos is apo tes thuseos tes psuches: imeros--oti eimenos pei e psuche: pothos, the desire which is in another place, allothi pou: eros was anciently esros, and so called because it flows into (esrei) the soul from without: doxa is e dioxis tou eidenai, or expresses the shooting from a bow (toxon). The latter etymology is confirmed by the words boulesthai, boule, aboulia, which all have to do with shooting (bole): and similarly oiesis is nothing but the movement (oisis) of the soul towards essence. Ekousion is to eikon--the yielding--anagke is e an agke iousa, the passage through ravines which impede motion: aletheia is theia ale, divine motion. Pseudos is the opposite of this, implying the principle of constraint and forced repose, which is expressed under the figure of sleep, to eudon; the psi is an addition. Onoma, a name, affirms the real existence of that which is sought after--on ou masma estin. On and ousia are only ion with an iota broken off; and ouk on is ouk ion. 'And what are ion, reon, doun?' One way of explaining them has been already suggested--they may be of foreign origin; and possibly this is the true answer. But mere antiquity may often prevent our recognizing words, after all the complications which they have undergone; and we must remember that however far we carry back our analysis some ultimate elements or roots will remain which can be no further analyzed. For example; the word agathos was supposed by us to be a compound of agastos and thoos, and probably thoos may be further resolvable. But if we take a word of which no further resolution seems attainable, we may fairly conclude that we have reached one of these original elements, and the truth of such a word must be tested by some new method. Will you help me in the search?

All names, whether primary or secondary, are intended to show the nature of things; and the secondary, as I conceive, derive their significance from the primary. But then, how do the primary names indicate anything? And let me ask another question,--If we had no faculty of speech, how should we communicate with one another? Should we not use signs, like the deaf and dumb? The elevation of our hands would mean lightness--heaviness would be expressed by letting them drop. The running of any animal would be described by a similar movement of our own frames. The body can only express anything by imitation; and the tongue or mouth can imitate as well as the rest of the body. But this imitation of the tongue or voice is not yet a name, because people may imitate sheep or goats without naming them. What, then, is a name? In the first place, a name is not a musical, or, secondly, a pictorial imitation, but an imitation of that kind which expresses the nature of a thing; and is the invention not of a musician, or of a painter, but of a namer.

And now, I think that we may consider the names about which you were asking. The way to analyze them will be by going back to the letters, or primary elements of which they are composed. First, we separate the alphabet into classes of letters, distinguishing the consonants, mutes, vowels, and semivowels; and when we have learnt them singly, we shall learn to know them in their various combinations of two or more letters; just as the painter knows how to use either a single colour, or a combination of colours. And like the painter, we may apply letters to the expression of objects, and form them into syllables; and these again into words, until the picture or figure--that is, language--is completed. Not that I am literally speaking of ourselves, but I mean to say that this was the way in which the ancients framed language. And this leads me to consider whether the primary as well as the secondary elements are rightly given. I may remark, as I was saying about the Gods, that we can only attain to conjecture of them. But still we insist that ours is the true and only method of discovery; otherwise we must have recourse, like the tragic poets, to a Deus ex machina, and say that God gave the first names, and therefore they are right; or that the barbarians are older than we are, and that we learnt of them; or that antiquity has cast a veil over the truth. Yet all these are not reasons; they are only ingenious excuses for having no reasons.

I will freely impart to you my own notions, though they are somewhat crude:--the letter rho appears to me to be the general instrument which the legislator has employed to express all motion or kinesis. (I ought to explain that kinesis is just iesis (going), for the letter eta was unknown to the ancients; and the root, kiein, is a foreign form of ienai: of kinesis or eisis, the opposite is stasis). This use of rho is evident in the words tremble, break, crush, crumble, and the like; the imposer of names perceived that the tongue is most agitated in the pronunciation of this letter, just as he used iota to express the subtle power which penetrates through all things. The letters phi, psi, sigma, zeta, which require a great deal of wind, are employed in the imitation of such notions as shivering, seething, shaking, and in general of what is windy. The letters delta and tau convey the idea of binding and rest in a place: the lambda denotes smoothness, as in the words slip, sleek, sleep, and the like. But when the slipping tongue is detained by the heavier sound of gamma, then arises the notion of a glutinous clammy nature: nu is sounded from within, and has a notion of inwardness: alpha is the expression of size; eta of length; omicron of roundness, and therefore there is plenty of omicron in the word goggulon. That is my view, Hermogenes, of the correctness of names; and I should like to hear what Cratylus would say. 'But, Socrates, as I was telling you, Cratylus mystifies me; I should like to ask him, in your presence, what he means by the fitness of names?' To this appeal, Cratylus replies 'that he cannot explain so important a subject all in a moment.' 'No, but you may "add little to little," as Hesiod says.' Socrates here interposes his own request, that Cratylus will give some account of his theory. Hermogenes and himself are mere sciolists, but Cratylus has reflected on these matters, and has had teachers. Cratylus replies in the words of Achilles: '"Illustrious Ajax, you have spoken in all things much to my mind," whether Euthyphro, or some Muse inhabiting your own breast, was the inspirer.' Socrates replies, that he is afraid of being self-deceived, and therefore he must 'look fore and aft,' as Homer remarks. Does not Cratylus agree with him that names teach us the nature of things? 'Yes.' And naming is an art, and the artists are legislators, and like artists in general, some of them are better and some of them are worse than others, and give better or worse laws, and make better or worse names. Cratylus cannot admit that one name is better than another; they are either true names, or they are not names at all; and when he is asked about the name of Hermogenes, who is acknowledged to have no luck in him, he affirms this to be the name of somebody else. Socrates supposes him to mean that falsehood is impossible, to which his own answer would be, that there has never been a lack of liars. Cratylus presses him with the old sophistical argument, that falsehood is saying that which is not, and therefore saying nothing;--you cannot utter the word which is not. Socrates complains that this argument is too subtle for an old man to understand: Suppose a person addressing Cratylus were to say, Hail, Athenian Stranger, Hermogenes! would these words be true or false? 'I should say that they would be mere unmeaning sounds, like the hammering of a brass pot.' But you would acknowledge that names, as well as pictures, are imitations, and also that pictures may give a right or wrong representation of a man or woman:--why may not names then equally give a representation true and right or false and wrong? Cratylus admits that pictures may give a true or false representation, but denies that names can. Socrates argues, that he may go up to a man and say 'this is year picture,' and again, he may go and say to him 'this is your name'--in the one case appealing to his sense of sight, and in the other to his sense of hearing;--may he not? 'Yes.' Then you will admit that there is a right or a wrong assignment of names, and if of names, then of verbs and nouns; and if of verbs and nouns, then of the sentences which are made up of them; and comparing nouns to pictures, you may give them all the appropriate sounds, or only some of them. And as he who gives all the colours makes a good picture, and he who gives only some of them, a bad or imperfect one, but still a picture; so he who gives all the sounds makes a good name, and he who gives only some of them, a bad or imperfect one, but a name still. The artist of names, that is, the legislator, may be a good or he may be a bad artist. 'Yes, Socrates, but the cases are not parallel; for if you subtract or misplace a letter, the name ceases to be a name.' Socrates admits that the number 10, if an unit is subtracted, would cease to be 10, but denies that names are of this purely quantitative nature. Suppose that there are two objects--Cratylus and the image of Cratylus; and let us imagine that some God makes them perfectly alike, both in their outward form and in their inner nature and qualities: then there will be two Cratyluses, and not merely Cratylus and the image of Cratylus. But an image in fact always falls short in some degree of the original, and if images are not exact counterparts, why should names be? if they were, they would be the doubles of their originals, and indistinguishable from them; and how ridiculous would this be! Cratylus admits the truth of Socrates' remark. But then Socrates rejoins, he should have the courage to acknowledge that letters may be wrongly inserted in a noun, or a noun in a sentence; and yet the noun or the sentence may retain a meaning. Better to admit this, that we may not be punished like the traveller in Egina who goes about at night, and that Truth herself may not say to us, 'Too late.' And, errors excepted, we may still affirm that a name to be correct must have proper letters, which bear a resemblance to the thing signified. I must remind you of what Hermogenes and I were saying about the letter rho accent, which was held to be expressive of motion and hardness, as lambda is of smoothness;--and this you will admit to be their natural meaning. But then, why do the Eritreans call that skleroter which we call sklerotes? We can understand one another, although the letter rho accent is not equivalent to the letter s: why is this? You reply, because the two letters are sufficiently alike for the purpose of expressing motion. Well, then, there is the letter lambda; what business has this in a word meaning hardness? 'Why, Socrates, I retort upon you, that we put in and pull out letters at pleasure.' And the explanation of this is custom or agreement: we have made a convention that the rho shall mean s and a convention may indicate by the unlike as well as by the like. How could there be names for all the numbers unless you allow that convention is used? Imitation is a poor thing, and has to be supplemented by convention, which is another poor thing; although I agree with you in thinking that the most perfect form of language is found only where there is a perfect correspondence of sound and meaning. But let me ask you what is the use and force of names? 'The use of names, Socrates, is to inform, and he who knows names knows things.' Do you mean that the discovery of names is the same as the discovery of things? 'Yes.' But do you not see that there is a degree of deception about names? He who first gave names, gave them according to his conception, and that may have been erroneous. 'But then, why, Socrates, is language so consistent? all words have the same laws.' Mere consistency is no test of truth. In geometrical problems, for example, there may be a flaw at the beginning, and yet the conclusion may follow consistently. And, therefore, a wise man will take especial care of first principles. But are words really consistent; are there not as many terms of praise which signify rest as which signify motion? There is episteme, which is connected with stasis, as mneme is with meno. Bebaion, again, is the expression of station and position; istoria is clearly descriptive of the stopping istanai of the stream; piston indicates the cessation of motion; and there are many words having a bad sense, which are connected with ideas of motion, such as sumphora, amartia, etc.: amathia, again, might be explained, as e ama theo iontos poreia, and akolasia as e akolouthia tois pragmasin. Thus the bad names are framed on the same principle as the good, and other examples might be given, which would favour a theory of rest rather than of motion. 'Yes; but the greater number of words express motion.' Are we to count them, Cratylus; and is correctness of names to be determined by the voice of a majority?

Here is another point: we were saying that the legislator gives names; and therefore we must suppose that he knows the things which he names: but how can he have learnt things from names before there were any names? 'I believe, Socrates, that some power more than human first gave things their names, and that these were necessarily true names.' Then how came the giver of names to contradict himself, and to make some names expressive of rest, and others of motion? 'I do not suppose that he did make them both.' Then which did he make--those which are expressive of rest, or those which are expressive of motion?...But if some names are true and others false, we can only decide between them, not by counting words, but by appealing to things. And, if so, we must allow that things may be known without names; for names, as we have several times admitted, are the images of things; and the higher knowledge is of things, and is not to be derived from names; and though I do not doubt that the inventors of language gave names, under the idea that all things are in a state of motion and flux, I believe that they were mistaken; and that having fallen into a whirlpool themselves, they are trying to drag us after them. For is there not a true beauty and a true good, which is always beautiful and always good? Can the thing beauty be vanishing away from us while the words are yet in our mouths? And they could not be known by any one if they are always passing away--for if they are always passing away, the observer has no opportunity of observing their state. Whether the doctrine of the flux or of the eternal nature be the truer, is hard to determine. But no man of sense will put himself, or the education of his mind, in the power of names: he will not condemn himself to be an unreal thing, nor will he believe that everything is in a flux like the water in a leaky vessel, or that the world is a man who has a running at the nose. This doctrine may be true, Cratylus, but is also very likely to be untrue; and therefore I would have you reflect while you are young, and find out the truth, and when you know come and tell me. 'I have thought, Socrates, and after a good deal of thinking I incline to Heracleitus.' Then another day, my friend, you shall give me a lesson. 'Very good, Socrates, and I hope that you will continue to study these things yourself.'

*****

 We may now consider (I) how far Plato in the Cratylus has discovered the true principles of language, and then (II) proceed to compare modern speculations respecting the origin and nature of language with the anticipations of his genius.

I. (1) Plato is aware that language is not the work of chance; nor does he deny that there is a natural fitness in names. He only insists that this natural fitness shall be intelligibly explained. But he has no idea that language is a natural organism. He would have heard with surprise that languages are the common work of whole nations in a primitive or semi-barbarous age. How, he would probably have argued, could men devoid of art have contrived a structure of such complexity? No answer could have been given to this question, either in ancient or in modern times, until the nature of primitive antiquity had been thoroughly studied, and the instincts of man had been shown to exist in greater force, when his state approaches more nearly to that of children or animals. The philosophers of the last century, after their manner, would have vainly endeavoured to trace the process by which proper names were converted into common, and would have shown how the last effort of abstraction invented prepositions and auxiliaries. The theologian would have proved that language must have had a divine origin, because in childhood, while the organs are pliable, the intelligence is wanting, and when the intelligence is able to frame conceptions, the organs are no longer able to express them. Or, as others have said: Man is man because he has the gift of speech; and he could not have invented that which he is. But this would have been an 'argument too subtle' for Socrates, who rejects the theological account of the origin of language 'as an excuse for not giving a reason,' which he compares to the introduction of the 'Deus ex machina' by the tragic poets when they have to solve a difficulty; thus anticipating many modern controversies in which the primary agency of the divine Being is confused with the secondary cause; and God is assumed to have worked a miracle in order to fill up a lacuna in human knowledge. (Compare Timaeus.)

Neither is Plato wrong in supposing that an element of design and art enters into language. The creative power abating is supplemented by a mechanical process. 'Languages are not made but grow,' but they are made as well as grow; bursting into life like a plant or a flower, they are also capable of being trained and improved and engrafted upon one another. The change in them is effected in earlier ages by musical and euphonic improvements, at a later stage by the influence of grammar and logic, and by the poetical and literary use of words. They develope rapidly in childhood, and when they are full grown and set they may still put forth intellectual powers, like the mind in the body, or rather we may say that the nobler use of language only begins when the frame-work is complete. The savage or primitive man, in whom the natural instinct is strongest, is also the greatest improver of the forms of language. He is the poet or maker of words, as in civilised ages the dialectician is the definer or distinguisher of them. The latter calls the second world of abstract terms into existence, as the former has created the picture sounds which represent natural objects or processes. Poetry and philosophy--these two, are the two great formative principles of language, when they have passed their first stage, of which, as of the first invention of the arts in general, we only entertain conjecture. And mythology is a link between them, connecting the visible and invisible, until at length the sensuous exterior falls away, and the severance of the inner and outer world, of the idea and the object of sense, becomes complete. At a later period, logic and grammar, sister arts, preserve and enlarge the decaying instinct of language, by rule and method, which they gather from analysis and observation.

(2) There is no trace in any of Plato's writings that he was acquainted with any language but Greek. Yet he has conceived very truly the relation of Greek to foreign languages, which he is led to consider, because he finds that many Greek words are incapable of explanation. Allowing a good deal for accident, and also for the fancies of the conditores linguae Graecae, there is an element of which he is unable to give an account. These unintelligible words he supposes to be of foreign origin, and to have been derived from a time when the Greeks were either barbarians, or in close relations to the barbarians. Socrates is aware that this principle is liable to great abuse; and, like the 'Deus ex machina,' explains nothing. Hence he excuses himself for the employment of such a device, and remarks that in foreign words there is still a principle of correctness, which applies equally both to Greeks and barbarians.

(3) But the greater number of primary words do not admit of derivation from foreign languages; they must be resolved into the letters out of which they are composed, and therefore the letters must have a meaning. The framers of language were aware of this; they observed that alpha was adapted to express size; eta length; omicron roundness; nu inwardness; rho accent rush or roar; lambda liquidity; gamma lambda the detention of the liquid or slippery element; delta and tau binding; phi, psi, sigma, xi, wind and cold, and so on. Plato's analysis of the letters of the alphabet shows a wonderful insight into the nature of language. He does not expressively distinguish between mere imitation and the symbolical use of sound to express thought, but he recognises in the examples which he gives both modes of imitation. Gesture is the mode which a deaf and dumb person would take of indicating his meaning. And language is the gesture of the tongue; in the use of the letter rho accent, to express a rushing or roaring, or of omicron to express roundness, there is a direct imitation; while in the use of the letter alpha to express size, or of eta to express length, the imitation is symbolical. The use of analogous or similar sounds, in order to express similar analogous ideas, seems to have escaped him.

In passing from the gesture of the body to the movement of the tongue, Plato makes a great step in the physiology of language. He was probably the first who said that 'language is imitative sound,' which is the greatest and deepest truth of philology; although he is not aware of the laws of euphony and association by which imitation must be regulated. He was probably also the first who made a distinction between simple and compound words, a truth second only in importance to that which has just been mentioned. His great insight in one direction curiously contrasts with his blindness in another; for he appears to be wholly unaware (compare his derivation of agathos from agastos and thoos) of the difference between the root and termination. But we must recollect that he was necessarily more ignorant than any schoolboy of Greek grammar, and had no table of the inflexions of verbs and nouns before his eyes, which might have suggested to him the distinction.

(4) Plato distinctly affirms that language is not truth, or 'philosophie une langue bien faite.' At first, Socrates has delighted himself with discovering the flux of Heracleitus in language. But he is covertly satirising the pretence of that or any other age to find philosophy in words; and he afterwards corrects any erroneous inference which might be gathered from his experiment. For he finds as many, or almost as many, words expressive of rest, as he had previously found expressive of motion. And even if this had been otherwise, who would learn of words when he might learn of things? There is a great controversy and high argument between Heracleiteans and Eleatics, but no man of sense would commit his soul in such enquiries to the imposers of names...In this and other passages Plato shows that he is as completely emancipated from the influence of 'Idols of the tribe' as Bacon himself.

The lesson which may be gathered from words is not metaphysical or moral, but historical. They teach us the affinity of races, they tell us something about the association of ideas, they occasionally preserve the memory of a disused custom; but we cannot safely argue from them about right and wrong, matter and mind, freedom and necessity, or the other problems of moral and metaphysical philosophy. For the use of words on such subjects may often be metaphorical, accidental, derived from other languages, and may have no relation to the contemporary state of thought and feeling. Nor in any case is the invention of them the result of philosophical reflection; they have been commonly transferred from matter to mind, and their meaning is the very reverse of their etymology. Because there is or is not a name for a thing, we cannot argue that the thing has or has not an actual existence; or that the antitheses, parallels, conjugates, correlatives of language have anything corresponding to them in nature. There are too many words as well as too few; and they generalize the objects or ideas which they represent. The greatest lesson which the philosophical analysis of language teaches us is, that we should be above language, making words our servants, and not allowing them to be our masters.

Plato does not add the further observation, that the etymological meaning of words is in process of being lost. If at first framed on a principle of intelligibility, they would gradually cease to be intelligible, like those of a foreign language, he is willing to admit that they are subject to many changes, and put on many disguises. He acknowledges that the 'poor creature' imitation is supplemented by another 'poor creature,'--convention. But he does not see that 'habit and repute,' and their relation to other words, are always exercising an influence over them. Words appear to be isolated, but they are really the parts of an organism which is always being reproduced. They are refined by civilization, harmonized by poetry, emphasized by literature, technically applied in philosophy and art; they are used as symbols on the border-ground of human knowledge; they receive a fresh impress from individual genius, and come with a new force and association to every lively-minded person. They are fixed by the simultaneous utterance of millions, and yet are always imperceptibly changing;--not the inventors of language, but writing and speaking, and particularly great writers, or works which pass into the hearts of nations, Homer, Shakespear, Dante, the German or English Bible, Kant and Hegel, are the makers of them in later ages. They carry with them the faded recollection of their own past history; the use of a word in a striking and familiar passage gives a complexion to its use everywhere else, and the new use of an old and familiar phrase has also a peculiar power over us. But these and other subtleties of language escaped the observation of Plato. He is not aware that the languages of the world are organic structures, and that every word in them is related to every other; nor does he conceive of language as the joint work of the speaker and the hearer, requiring in man a faculty not only of expressing his thoughts but of understanding those of others.

On the other hand, he cannot be justly charged with a desire to frame language on artificial principles. Philosophers have sometimes dreamed of a technical or scientific language, in words which should have fixed meanings, and stand in the same relation to one another as the substances which they denote. But there is no more trace of this in Plato than there is of a language corresponding to the ideas; nor, indeed, could the want of such a language be felt until the sciences were far more developed. Those who would extend the use of technical phraseology beyond the limits of science or of custom, seem to forget that freedom and suggestiveness and the play of association are essential characteristics of language. The great master has shown how he regarded pedantic distinctions of words or attempts to confine their meaning in the satire on Prodicus in the Protagoras.

(5) In addition to these anticipations of the general principles of philology, we may note also a few curious observations on words and sounds. 'The Eretrians say sklerotes for skleroter;' 'the Thessalians call Apollo Amlos;' 'The Phrygians have the words pur, udor, kunes slightly changed;' 'there is an old Homeric word emesato, meaning "he contrived";' 'our forefathers, and especially the women, who are most conservative of the ancient language, loved the letters iota and delta; but now iota is changed into eta and epsilon, and delta into zeta; this is supposed to increase the grandeur of the sound.' Plato was very willing to use inductive arguments, so far as they were within his reach; but he would also have assigned a large influence to chance. Nor indeed is induction applicable to philology in the same degree as to most of the physical sciences. For after we have pushed our researches to the furthest point, in language as in all the other creations of the human mind, there will always remain an element of exception or accident or free-will, which cannot be eliminated.

The question, 'whether falsehood is impossible,' which Socrates characteristically sets aside as too subtle for an old man (compare Euthyd.), could only have arisen in an age of imperfect consciousness, which had not yet learned to distinguish words from things. Socrates replies in effect that words have an independent existence; thus anticipating the solution of the mediaeval controversy of Nominalism and Realism. He is aware too that languages exist in various degrees of perfection, and that the analysis of them can only be carried to a certain point. 'If we could always, or almost always, use likenesses, which are the appropriate expressions, that would be the most perfect state of language.' These words suggest a question of deeper interest than the origin of language; viz. what is the ideal of language, how far by any correction of their usages existing languages might become clearer and more expressive than they are, more poetical, and also more logical; or whether they are now finally fixed and have received their last impress from time and authority.

On the whole, the Cratylus seems to contain deeper truths about language than any other ancient writing. But feeling the uncertain ground upon which he is walking, and partly in order to preserve the character of Socrates, Plato envelopes the whole subject in a robe of fancy, and allows his principles to drop out as if by accident.

II. What is the result of recent speculations about the origin and nature of language? Like other modern metaphysical enquiries, they end at last in a statement of facts. But, in order to state or understand the facts, a metaphysical insight seems to be required. There are more things in language than the human mind easily conceives. And many fallacies have to be dispelled, as well as observations made. The true spirit of philosophy or metaphysics can alone charm away metaphysical illusions, which are always reappearing, formerly in the fancies of neoplatonist writers, now in the disguise of experience and common sense. An analogy, a figure of speech, an intelligible theory, a superficial observation of the individual, have often been mistaken for a true account of the origin of language.

Speaking is one of the simplest natural operations, and also the most complex. Nothing would seem to be easier or more trivial than a few words uttered by a child in any language. Yet into the formation of those words have entered causes which the human mind is not capable of calculating. They are a drop or two of the great stream or ocean of speech which has been flowing in all ages. They have been transmitted from one language to another; like the child himself, they go back to the beginnings of the human race. How they originated, who can tell? Nevertheless we can imagine a stage of human society in which the circle of men's minds was narrower and their sympathies and instincts stronger; in which their organs of speech were more flexible, and the sense of hearing finer and more discerning; in which they lived more in company, and after the manner of children were more given to express their feelings; in which 'they moved all together,' like a herd of wild animals, 'when they moved at all.' Among them, as in every society, a particular person would be more sensitive and intelligent than the rest. Suddenly, on some occasion of interest (at the approach of a wild beast, shall we say?), he first, they following him, utter a cry which resounds through the forest. The cry is almost or quite involuntary, and may be an imitation of the roar of the animal. Thus far we have not speech, but only the inarticulate expression of feeling or emotion in no respect differing from the cries of animals; for they too call to one another and are answered. But now suppose that some one at a distance not only hears the sound, but apprehends the meaning: or we may imagine that the cry is repeated to a member of the society who had been absent; the others act the scene over again when he returns home in the evening. And so the cry becomes a word. The hearer in turn gives back the word to the speaker, who is now aware that he has acquired a new power. Many thousand times he exercises this power; like a child learning to talk, he repeats the same cry again, and again he is answered; he tries experiments with a like result, and the speaker and the hearer rejoice together in their newly-discovered faculty. At first there would be few such cries, and little danger of mistaking or confusing them. For the mind of primitive man had a narrow range of perceptions and feelings; his senses were microscopic; twenty or thirty sounds or gestures would be enough for him, nor would he have any difficulty in finding them. Naturally he broke out into speech--like the young infant he laughed and babbled; but not until there were hearers as well as speakers did language begin. Not the interjection or the vocal imitation of the object, but the interjection or the vocal imitation of the object understood, is the first rudiment of human speech.

After a while the word gathers associations, and has an independent existence. The imitation of the lion's roar calls up the fears and hopes of the chase, which are excited by his appearance. In the moment of hearing the sound, without any appreciable interval, these and other latent experiences wake up in the mind of the hearer. Not only does he receive an impression, but he brings previous knowledge to bear upon that impression. Necessarily the pictorial image becomes less vivid, while the association of the nature and habits of the animal is more distinctly perceived. The picture passes into a symbol, for there would be too many of them and they would crowd the mind; the vocal imitation, too, is always in process of being lost and being renewed, just as the picture is brought back again in the description of the poet. Words now can be used more freely because there are more of them. What was once an involuntary expression becomes voluntary. Not only can men utter a cry or call, but they can communicate and converse; they can not only use words, but they can even play with them. The word is separated both from the object and from the mind; and slowly nations and individuals attain to a fuller consciousness of themselves.

Parallel with this mental process the articulation of sounds is gradually becoming perfected. The finer sense detects the differences of them, and begins, first to agglomerate, then to distinguish them. Times, persons, places, relations of all kinds, are expressed by modifications of them. The earliest parts of speech, as we may call them by anticipation, like the first utterances of children, probably partook of the nature of interjections and nouns; then came verbs; at length the whole sentence appeared, and rhythm and metre followed. Each stage in the progress of language was accompanied by some corresponding stage in the mind and civilisation of man. In time, when the family became a nation, the wild growth of dialects passed into a language. Then arose poetry and literature. We can hardly realize to ourselves how much with each improvement of language the powers of the human mind were enlarged; how the inner world took the place of outer; how the pictorial or symbolical or analogical word was refined into a notion; how language, fair and large and free, was at last complete.

So we may imagine the speech of man to have begun as with the cries of animals, or the stammering lips of children, and to have attained by degrees the perfection of Homer and Plato. Yet we are far from saying that this or any other theory of language is proved by facts. It is not difficult to form an hypothesis which by a series of imaginary transitions will bridge over the chasm which separates man from the animals. Differences of kind may often be thus resolved into differences of degree. But we must not assume that we have in this way discovered the true account of them. Through what struggles the harmonious use of the organs of speech was acquired; to what extent the conditions of human life were different; how far the genius of individuals may have contributed to the discovery of this as of the other arts, we cannot say: Only we seem to see that language is as much the creation of the ear as of the tongue, and the expression of a movement stirring the hearts not of one man only but of many, 'as the trees of the wood are stirred by the wind.' The theory is consistent or not inconsistent with our own mental experience, and throws some degree of light upon a dark corner of the human mind.

In the later analysis of language, we trace the opposite and contrasted elements of the individual and nation, of the past and present, of the inward and outward, of the subject and object, of the notional and relational, of the root or unchanging part of the word and of the changing inflexion, if such a distinction be admitted, of the vowel and the consonant, of quantity and accent, of speech and writing, of poetry and prose. We observe also the reciprocal influence of sounds and conceptions on each other, like the connexion of body and mind; and further remark that although the names of objects were originally proper names, as the grammarian or logician might call them, yet at a later stage they become universal notions, which combine into particulars and individuals, and are taken out of the first rude agglomeration of sounds that they may be replaced in a higher and more logical order. We see that in the simplest sentences are contained grammar and logic--the parts of speech, the Eleatic philosophy and the Kantian categories. So complex is language, and so expressive not only of the meanest wants of man, but of his highest thoughts; so various are the aspects in which it is regarded by us. Then again, when we follow the history of languages, we observe that they are always slowly moving, half dead, half alive, half solid, half fluid; the breath of a moment, yet like the air, continuous in all ages and countries,-- like the glacier, too, containing within them a trickling stream which deposits debris of the rocks over which it passes. There were happy moments, as we may conjecture, in the lives of nations, at which they came to the birth--as in the golden age of literature, the man and the time seem to conspire; the eloquence of the bard or chief, as in later times the creations of the great writer who is the expression of his age, became impressed on the minds of their countrymen, perhaps in the hour of some crisis of national development--a migration, a conquest, or the like. The picture of the word which was beginning to be lost, is now revived; the sound again echoes to the sense; men find themselves capable not only of expressing more feelings, and describing more objects, but of expressing and describing them better. The world before the flood, that is to say, the world of ten, twenty, a hundred thousand years ago, has passed away and left no sign. But the best conception that we can form of it, though imperfect and uncertain, is gained from the analogy of causes still in action, some powerful and sudden, others working slowly in the course of infinite ages. Something too may be allowed to 'the persistency of the strongest,' to 'the survival of the fittest,' in this as in the other realms of nature.

These are some of the reflections which the modern philosophy of language suggests to us about the powers of the human mind and the forces and influences by which the efforts of men to utter articulate sounds were inspired. Yet in making these and similar generalizations we may note also dangers to which we are exposed. (1) There is the confusion of ideas with facts--of mere possibilities, and generalities, and modes of conception with actual and definite knowledge. The words 'evolution,' 'birth,' 'law,' development,' 'instinct,' 'implicit,' 'explicit,' and the like, have a false clearness or comprehensiveness, which adds nothing to our knowledge. The metaphor of a flower or a tree, or some other work of nature or art, is often in like manner only a pleasing picture. (2) There is the fallacy of resolving the languages which we know into their parts, and then imagining that we can discover the nature of language by reconstructing them. (3) There is the danger of identifying language, not with thoughts but with ideas. (4) There is the error of supposing that the analysis of grammar and logic has always existed, or that their distinctions were familiar to Socrates and Plato. (5) There is the fallacy of exaggerating, and also of diminishing the interval which separates articulate from inarticulate language-- the cries of animals from the speech of man--the instincts of animals from the reason of man. (6) There is the danger which besets all enquiries into the early history of man--of interpreting the past by the present, and of substituting the definite and intelligible for the true but dim outline which is the horizon of human knowledge.

The greatest light is thrown upon the nature of language by analogy. We have the analogy of the cries of animals, of the songs of birds ('man, like the nightingale, is a singing bird, but is ever binding up thoughts with musical notes'), of music, of children learning to speak, of barbarous nations in which the linguistic instinct is still undecayed, of ourselves learning to think and speak a new language, of the deaf and dumb who have words without sounds, of the various disorders of speech; and we have the after-growth of mythology, which, like language, is an unconscious creation of the human mind. We can observe the social and collective instincts of animals, and may remark how, when domesticated, they have the power of understanding but not of speaking, while on the other hand, some birds which are comparatively devoid of intelligence, make a nearer approach to articulate speech. We may note how in the animals there is a want of that sympathy with one another which appears to be the soul of language. We can compare the use of speech with other mental and bodily operations; for speech too is a kind of gesture, and in the child or savage accompanied with gesture. We may observe that the child learns to speak, as he learns to walk or to eat, by a natural impulse; yet in either case not without a power of imitation which is also natural to him--he is taught to read, but he breaks forth spontaneously in speech. We can trace the impulse to bind together the world in ideas beginning in the first efforts to speak and culminating in philosophy. But there remains an element which cannot be explained, or even adequately described. We can understand how man creates or constructs consciously and by design; and see, if we do not understand, how nature, by a law, calls into being an organised structure. But the intermediate organism which stands between man and nature, which is the work of mind yet unconscious, and in which mind and matter seem to meet, and mind unperceived to herself is really limited by all other minds, is neither understood nor seen by us, and is with reluctance admitted to be a fact.

Language is an aspect of man, of nature, and of nations, the transfiguration of the world in thought, the meeting-point of the physical and mental sciences, and also the mirror in which they are reflected, present at every moment to the individual, and yet having a sort of eternal or universal nature. When we analyze our own mental processes, we find words everywhere in every degree of clearness and consistency, fading away in dreams and more like pictures, rapidly succeeding one another in our waking thoughts, attaining a greater distinctness and consecutiveness in speech, and a greater still in writing, taking the place of one another when we try to become emancipated from their influence. For in all processes of the mind which are conscious we are talking to ourselves; the attempt to think without words is a mere illusion,--they are always reappearing when we fix our thoughts. And speech is not a separate faculty, but the expression of all our faculties, to which all our other powers of expression, signs, looks, gestures, lend their aid, of which the instrument is not the tongue only, but more than half the human frame.

The minds of men are sometimes carried on to think of their lives and of their actions as links in a chain of causes and effects going back to the beginning of time. A few have seemed to lose the sense of their own individuality in the universal cause or nature. In like manner we might think of the words which we daily use, as derived from the first speech of man, and of all the languages in the world, as the expressions or varieties of a single force or life of language of which the thoughts of men are the accident. Such a conception enables us to grasp the power and wonder of languages, and is very natural to the scientific philologist. For he, like the metaphysician, believes in the reality of that which absorbs his own mind. Nor do we deny the enormous influence which language has exercised over thought. Fixed words, like fixed ideas, have often governed the world. But in such representations we attribute to language too much the nature of a cause, and too little of an effect,--too much of an absolute, too little of a relative character,--too much of an ideal, too little of a matter-of-fact existence.

Or again, we may frame a single abstract notion of language of which all existent languages may be supposed to be the perversion. But we must not conceive that this logical figment had ever a real existence, or is anything more than an effort of the mind to give unity to infinitely various phenomena. There is no abstract language 'in rerum natura,' any more than there is an abstract tree, but only languages in various stages of growth, maturity, and decay. Nor do other logical distinctions or even grammatical exactly correspond to the facts of language; for they too are attempts to give unity and regularity to a subject which is partly irregular.

We find, however, that there are distinctions of another kind by which this vast field of language admits of being mapped out. There is the distinction between biliteral and triliteral roots, and the various inflexions which accompany them; between the mere mechanical cohesion of sounds or words, and the 'chemical' combination of them into a new word; there is the distinction between languages which have had a free and full development of their organisms, and languages which have been stunted in their growth,--lamed in their hands or feet, and never able to acquire afterwards the powers in which they are deficient; there is the distinction between synthetical languages like Greek and Latin, which have retained their inflexions, and analytical languages like English or French, which have lost them. Innumerable as are the languages and dialects of mankind, there are comparatively few classes to which they can be referred.

Another road through this chaos is provided by the physiology of speech. The organs of language are the same in all mankind, and are only capable of uttering a certain number of sounds. Every man has tongue, teeth, lips, palate, throat, mouth, which he may close or open, and adapt in various ways; making, first, vowels and consonants; and secondly, other classes of letters. The elements of all speech, like the elements of the musical scale, are few and simple, though admitting of infinite gradations and combinations. Whatever slight differences exist in the use or formation of these organs, owing to climate or the sense of euphony or other causes, they are as nothing compared with their agreement. Here then is a real basis of unity in the study of philology, unlike that imaginary abstract unity of which we were just now speaking.

Whether we regard language from the psychological, or historical, or physiological point of view, the materials of our knowledge are inexhaustible. The comparisons of children learning to speak, of barbarous nations, of musical notes, of the cries of animals, of the song of birds, increase our insight into the nature of human speech. Many observations which would otherwise have escaped us are suggested by them. But they do not explain why, in man and in man only, the speaker met with a response from the hearer, and the half articulate sound gradually developed into Sanscrit and Greek. They hardly enable us to approach any nearer the secret of the origin of language, which, like some of the other great secrets of nature,--the origin of birth and death, or of animal life,--remains inviolable. That problem is indissolubly bound up with the origin of man; and if we ever know more of the one, we may expect to know more of the other. (Compare W. Humboldt, 'Ueber die Verschiedenheit des menschlichen Sprachbaues;' M. Muller, 'Lectures on the Science of Language;' Steinthal, 'Einleitung in die Psychologie und Sprachwissenschaft.')

*****

It is more than sixteen years since the preceding remarks were written, which with a few alterations have now been reprinted. During the interval the progress of philology has been very great. More languages have been compared; the inner structure of language has been laid bare; the relations of sounds have been more accurately discriminated; the manner in which dialects affect or are affected by the literary or principal form of a language is better understood. Many merely verbal questions have been eliminated; the remains of the old traditional methods have died away. The study has passed from the metaphysical into an historical stage. Grammar is no longer confused with language, nor the anatomy of words and sentences with their life and use. Figures of speech, by which the vagueness of theories is often concealed, have been stripped off; and we see language more as it truly was. The immensity of the subject is gradually revealed to us, and the reign of law becomes apparent. Yet the law is but partially seen; the traces of it are often lost in the distance. For languages have a natural but not a perfect growth; like other creations of nature into which the will of man enters, they are full of what we term accident and irregularity. And the difficulties of the subject become not less, but greater, as we proceed--it is one of those studies in which we seem to know less as we know more; partly because we are no longer satisfied with the vague and superficial ideas of it which prevailed fifty years ago; partly also because the remains of the languages with which we are acquainted always were, and if they are still living, are, in a state of transition; and thirdly, because there are lacunae in our knowledge of them which can never be filled up. Not a tenth, not a hundredth part of them has been preserved. Yet the materials at our disposal are far greater than any individual can use. Such are a few of the general reflections which the present state of philology calls up.

(1) Language seems to be composite, but into its first elements the philologer has never been able to penetrate. However far he goes back, he never arrives at the beginning; or rather, as in Geology or in Astronomy, there is no beginning. He is too apt to suppose that by breaking up the existing forms of language into their parts he will arrive at a previous stage of it, but he is merely analyzing what never existed, or is never known to have existed, except in a composite form. He may divide nouns and verbs into roots and inflexions, but he has no evidence which will show that the omega of tupto or the mu of tithemi, though analogous to ego, me, either became pronouns or were generated out of pronouns. To say that 'pronouns, like ripe fruit, dropped out of verbs,' is a misleading figure of speech. Although all languages have some common principles, there is no primitive form or forms of language known to us, or to be reasonably imagined, from which they are all descended. No inference can be drawn from language, either for or against the unity of the human race. Nor is there any proof that words were ever used without any relation to each other. Whatever may be the meaning of a sentence or a word when

applied to primitive language, it is probable that the sentence is more akin to the original form than the word, and that the later stage of language is the result rather of analysis than of synthesis, or possibly is a combination of the two. Nor, again, are we sure that the original process of learning to speak was the same in different places or among different races of men. It may have been slower with some, quicker with others. Some tribes may have used shorter, others longer words or cries: they may have been more or less inclined to agglutinate or to decompose them: they may have modified them by the use of prefixes, suffixes, infixes; by the lengthening and strengthening of vowels or by the shortening and weakening of them, by the condensation or rarefaction of consonants. But who gave to language these primeval laws; or why one race has triliteral, another biliteral roots; or why in some members of a group of languages b becomes p, or d, t, or ch, k; or why two languages resemble one another in certain parts of their structure and differ in others; or why in one language there is a greater development of vowels, in another of consonants, and the like--are questions of which we only 'entertain conjecture.' We must remember the length of time that has elapsed since man first walked upon the earth, and that in this vast but unknown period every variety of language may have been in process of formation and decay, many times over.

(Compare Plato, Laws):--

'ATHENIAN STRANGER: And what then is to be regarded as the origin of government? Will not a man be able to judge best from a point of view in which he may behold the progress of states and their transitions to good and evil?

CLEINIAS: What do you mean?

ATHENIAN STRANGER: I mean that he might watch them from the point of view of time, and observe the changes which take place in them during infinite ages.

CLEINIAS: How so?

ATHENIAN STRANGER: Why, do you think that you can reckon the time which has elapsed since cities first existed and men were citizens of them?

CLEINIAS: Hardly.

ATHENIAN STRANGER: But you are quite sure that it must be vast and incalculable?

CLEINIAS: No doubt.

ATHENIAN STRANGER: And have there not been thousands and thousands of cities which have come into being and perished during this period? And has not every place had endless forms of government, and been sometimes rising, and at other times falling, and again improving or waning?'

Aristot. Metaph.:--

'And if a person should conceive the tales of mythology to mean only that men thought the gods to be the first essences of things, he would deem the reflection to have been inspired and would consider that, whereas probably every art and part of wisdom had been DISCOVERED AND LOST MANY TIMES OVER, such notions were but a remnant of the past which has survived to our day.')

It can hardly be supposed that any traces of an original language still survive, any more than of the first huts or buildings which were constructed by man. Nor are we at all certain of the relation, if any, in which the greater families of languages stand to each other. The influence of individuals must always have been a disturbing element. Like great writers in later times, there may have been many a barbaric genius who taught the men of his tribe to sing or speak, showing them by example how to continue or divide their words, charming their souls with rhythm and accent and intonation, finding in familiar objects the expression of their confused fancies--to whom the whole of language might in truth be said to be a figure of speech. One person may have introduced a new custom into the formation or pronunciation of a word; he may have been imitated by others, and the custom, or form, or accent, or quantity, or rhyme which he introduced in a single word may have become the type on which many other words or inflexions of words were framed, and may have quickly ran through a whole language. For like the other gifts which nature has bestowed upon man, that of speech has been conveyed to him through the medium, not of the many, but of the few, who were his 'law-givers'--'the legislator with the dialectician standing on his right hand,' in Plato's striking image, who formed the manners of men and gave them customs, whose voice and look and behaviour, whose gesticulations and other peculiarities were instinctively imitated by them,--the 'king of men' who was their priest, almost their God...But these are conjectures only: so little do we know of the origin of language that the real scholar is indisposed to touch the subject at all.

(2) There are other errors besides the figment of a primitive or original language which it is time to leave behind us. We no longer divide languages into synthetical and analytical, or suppose similarity of structure to be the safe or only guide to the affinities of them. We do not confuse the parts of speech with the categories of Logic. Nor do we conceive languages any more than civilisations to be in a state of dissolution; they do not easily pass away, but are far more tenacious of life than the tribes by whom they are spoken. 'Where two or three are gathered together,' they survive. As in the human frame, as in the state, there is a principle of renovation as well as of decay which is at work in all of them. Neither do we suppose them to be invented by the wit of man. With few exceptions, e.g. technical words or words newly imported from a foreign language, and the like, in which art has imitated nature, 'words are not made but grow.' Nor do we attribute to them a supernatural origin. The law which regulates them is like the law which governs the circulation of the blood, or the rising of the sap in trees; the action of it is uniform, but the result, which appears in the superficial forms of men and animals or in the leaves of trees, is an endless profusion and variety. The laws of vegetation are invariable, but no two plants, no two leaves of the forest are precisely the same. The laws of language are invariable, but no two languages are alike, no two words have exactly the same meaning. No two sounds are exactly of the same quality, or give precisely the same impression.

It would be well if there were a similar consensus about some other points which appear to be still in dispute. Is language conscious or unconscious? In speaking or writing have we present to our minds the meaning or the sound or the construction of the words which we are using?--No more than the separate drops of water with which we quench our thirst are present: the whole draught may be conscious, but not the minute particles of which it is made up: So the whole sentence may be conscious, but the several words, syllables, letters are not thought of separately when we are uttering them. Like other natural operations, the process of speech, when most perfect, is least observed by us. We do not pause at each mouthful to dwell upon the taste of it: nor has the speaker time to ask himself the comparative merits of different modes of expression while he is uttering them. There are many things in the use of language which may be observed from without, but which cannot be explained from within. Consciousness carries us but a little way in the investigation of the mind; it is not the faculty of internal observation, but only the dim light which makes such observation possible. What is supposed to be our consciousness of language is really only the analysis of it, and this analysis admits of innumerable degrees. But would it not be better if this term, which is so misleading, and yet has played so great a part in mental science, were either banished or used only with the distinct meaning of 'attention to our own minds,' such as is called forth, not by familiar mental processes, but by the interruption of them? Now in this sense we may truly say that we are not conscious of ordinary speech, though we are commonly roused to attention by the misuse or mispronunciation of a word. Still less, even in schools and academies, do we ever attempt to invent new words or to alter the meaning of old ones, except in the case, mentioned above, of technical or borrowed words which are artificially made or imported because a need of them is felt. Neither in our own nor in any other age has the conscious effort of reflection in man contributed in an appreciable degree to the formation of language. 'Which of us by taking thought' can make new words or constructions? Reflection is the least of the causes by which language is affected, and is likely to have the least power, when the linguistic instinct is greatest, as in young children and in the infancy of nations.

A kindred error is the separation of the phonetic from the mental element of language; they are really inseparable--no definite line can be drawn between them, any more than in any other common act of mind and body. It is true that within certain limits we possess the power of varying sounds by opening and closing the mouth, by touching the palate or the teeth with the tongue, by lengthening or shortening the vocal instrument, by greater or less stress, by a higher or lower pitch of the voice, and we can substitute one note or accent for another. But behind the organs of speech and their action there remains the informing mind, which sets them in motion and works together with them. And behind the great structure of human speech and the lesser varieties of language which arise out of the many degrees and kinds of human intercourse, there is also the unknown or over-ruling law of God or nature which gives order to it in its infinite greatness, and variety in its infinitesimal minuteness--both equally inscrutable to us. We need no longer discuss whether philology is to be classed with the Natural or the Mental sciences, if we frankly recognize that, like all the sciences which are concerned with man, it has a double aspect,--inward and outward; and that the inward can only be known through the outward. Neither need we raise the question whether the laws of language, like the other laws of human action, admit of exceptions. The answer in all cases is the same--that the laws of nature are uniform, though the consistency or continuity of them is not always perceptible to us. The superficial appearances of language, as of nature, are irregular, but we do not therefore deny their deeper uniformity. The comparison of the growth of language in the individual and in the nation cannot be wholly discarded, for nations are made up of individuals. But in this, as in the other political sciences, we must distinguish between collective and individual actions or processes, and not attribute to the one what belongs to the other. Again, when we speak of the hereditary or paternity of a language, we must remember that the parents are alive as well as the children, and that all the preceding generations survive (after a manner) in the latest form of it. And when, for the purposes of comparison, we form into groups the roots or terminations of words, we should not forget how casual is the manner in which their resemblances have arisen--they were not first written down by a grammarian in the paradigms of a grammar and learned out of a book, but were due to many chance attractions of sound or of meaning, or of both combined. So many cautions have to be borne in mind, and so many first thoughts to be dismissed, before we can proceed safely in the path of philological enquiry. It might be well sometimes to lay aside figures of speech, such as the 'root' and the 'branches,' the 'stem,' the 'strata' of Geology, the 'compounds' of Chemistry, 'the ripe fruit of pronouns dropping from verbs' (see above), and the like, which are always interesting, but are apt to be delusive. Yet such figures of speech are far nearer the truth than the theories which attribute the invention and improvement of language to the conscious action of the human mind...Lastly, it is doubted by recent philologians whether climate can be supposed to have exercised any influence worth speaking of on a language: such a view is said to be unproven: it had better therefore not be silently assumed.

'Natural selection' and the 'survival of the fittest' have been applied in the field of philology, as well as in the other sciences which are concerned with animal and vegetable life. And a Darwinian school of philologists has sprung up, who are sometimes accused of putting words in the place of things. It seems to be true, that whether applied to language or to other branches of knowledge, the Darwinian theory, unless very precisely defined, hardly escapes from being a truism. If by 'the natural selection' of words or meanings of words or by the 'persistence and survival of the fittest' the maintainer of the theory intends to affirm nothing more than this--that the word 'fittest to survive' survives, he adds not much to the knowledge of language. But if he means that the word or the meaning of the word or some portion of the word which comes into use or drops out of use is selected or rejected on the ground of economy or parsimony or ease to the speaker or clearness or euphony or expressiveness, or greater or less demand for it, or anything of this sort, he is affirming a proposition which has several senses, and in none of these senses can be assisted to be uniformly true. For the laws of language are precarious, and can only act uniformly when there is such frequency of intercourse among neighbours as is sufficient to enforce them. And there are many reasons why a man should prefer his own way of speaking to that of others, unless by so doing he becomes unintelligible. The struggle for existence among words is not of that fierce and irresistible kind in which birds, beasts and fishes devour one another, but of a milder sort, allowing one usage to be substituted for another, not by force, but by the persuasion, or rather by the prevailing habit, of a majority. The favourite figure, in this, as in some other uses of it, has tended rather to obscure than explain the subject to which it has been applied. Nor in any case can the struggle for existence be deemed to be the sole or principal cause of changes in language, but only one among many, and one of which we cannot easily measure the importance. There is a further objection which may be urged equally against all applications of the Darwinian theory. As in animal life and likewise in vegetable, so in languages, the process of change is said to be insensible: sounds, like animals, are supposed to pass into one another by imperceptible gradation. But in both cases the newly-created forms soon become fixed; there are few if any vestiges of the intermediate links, and so the better half of the evidence of the change is wanting.

(3) Among the incumbrances or illusions of language may be reckoned many of the rules and traditions of grammar, whether ancient grammar or the corrections of it which modern philology has introduced. Grammar, like law, delights in definition: human speech, like human action, though very far from being a mere chaos, is indefinite, admits of degrees, and is always in a state of change or transition. Grammar gives an erroneous conception of language: for it reduces to a system that which is not a system. Its figures of speech, pleonasms, ellipses, anacolutha, pros to semainomenon, and the like have no reality; they do not either make conscious expressions more intelligible or show the way in which they have arisen; they are chiefly designed to bring an earlier use of language into conformity with the later. Often they seem intended only to remind us that great poets like Aeschylus or Sophocles or Pindar or a great prose writer like Thucydides are guilty of taking unwarrantable liberties with grammatical rules; it appears never to have occurred to the inventors of them that these real 'conditores linguae Graecae' lived in an age before grammar, when 'Greece also was living Greece.' It is the anatomy, not the physiology of language, which grammar seeks to describe: into the idiom and higher life of words it does not enter. The ordinary Greek grammar gives a complete paradigm of the verb, without suggesting that the double or treble forms of Perfects, Aorists, etc. are hardly ever contemporaneous. It distinguishes Moods and Tenses, without observing how much of the nature of one passes into the other. It makes three Voices, Active, Passive, and Middle, but takes no notice of the precarious existence and uncertain character of the last of the three. Language is a thing of degrees and relations and associations and

exceptions: grammar ties it up in fixed rules. Language has many varieties of usage: grammar tries to reduce them to a single one. Grammar divides verbs into regular and irregular: it does not recognize that the irregular, equally with the regular, are subject to law, and that a language which had no exceptions would not be a natural growth: for it could not have been subjected to the influences by which language is ordinarily affected. It is always wanting to describe ancient languages in the terms of a modern one. It has a favourite fiction that one word is put in the place of another; the truth is that no word is ever put for another. It has another fiction, that a word has been omitted: words are omitted because they are no longer needed; and the omission has ceased to be observed. The common explanation of kata or some other preposition 'being understood' in a Greek sentence is another fiction of the same kind, which tends to disguise the fact that under cases were comprehended originally many more relations, and that prepositions are used only to define the meaning of them with greater precision. These instances are sufficient to show the sort of errors which grammar introduces into language. We are not considering the question of its utility to the beginner in the study. Even to him the best grammar is the shortest and that in which he will have least to unlearn. It may be said that the explanations here referred to are already out of date, and that the study of Greek grammar has received a new character from comparative philology. This is true; but it is also true that the traditional grammar has still a great hold on the mind of the student.

Metaphysics are even more troublesome than the figments of grammar, because they wear the appearance of philosophy and there is no test to which they can be subjected. They are useful in so far as they give us an insight into the history of the human mind and the modes of thought which have existed in former ages; or in so far as they furnish wider conceptions of the different branches of knowledge and of their relation to one another. But they are worse than useless when they outrun experience and abstract the mind from the observation of facts, only to envelope it in a mist of words. Some philologers, like Schleicher, have been greatly influenced by the philosophy of Hegel; nearly all of them to a certain extent have fallen under the dominion of physical science. Even Kant himself thought that the first principles of philosophy could be elicited from the analysis of the proposition, in this respect falling short of Plato. Westphal holds that there are three stages of language: (1) in which things were characterized independently, (2) in which they were regarded in relation to human thought, and (3) in relation to one another. But are not such distinctions an anachronism? for they imply a growth of abstract ideas which never existed in early times. Language cannot be explained by Metaphysics; for it is prior to them and much more nearly allied to sense. It is not likely that the meaning of the cases is ultimately resolvable into relations of space and time. Nor can we suppose the conception of cause and effect or of the finite and infinite or of the same and other to be latent in language at a time when in their abstract form they had never entered into the mind of man...If the science of Comparative Philology had possessed 'enough of Metaphysics to get rid of Metaphysics,' it would have made far greater progress.

(4) Our knowledge of language is almost confined to languages which are fully developed. They are of several patterns; and these become altered by admixture in various degrees,--they may only borrow a few words from one another and retain their life comparatively unaltered, or they may meet in a struggle for existence until one of the two is overpowered and retires from the field. They attain the full rights and dignity of language when they acquire the use of writing and have a literature of their own; they pass into dialects and grow out of them, in proportion as men are isolated or united by locality or occupation. The common language sometimes reacts upon the dialects and imparts to them also a literary character. The laws of language can be best discerned in the great crises of language, especially in the transitions from ancient to modern forms of them, whether in Europe or Asia. Such changes are the silent notes of the world's history; they mark periods of unknown length in which war and conquest

were running riot over whole continents, times of suffering too great to be endured by the human race, in which the masters became subjects and the subject races masters, in which driven by necessity or impelled by some instinct, tribes or nations left their original homes and but slowly found a resting-place. Language would be the greatest of all historical monuments, if it could only tell us the history of itself.

(5) There are many ways in which we may approach this study. The simplest of all is to observe our own use of language in conversation or in writing, how we put words together, how we construct and connect sentences, what are the rules of accent and rhythm in verse or prose, the formation and composition of words, the laws of euphony and sound, the affinities of letters, the mistakes to which we are ourselves most liable of spelling or pronunciation. We may compare with our own language some other, even when we have only a slight knowledge of it, such as French or German. Even a little Latin will enable us to appreciate the grand difference between ancient and modern European languages. In the child learning to speak we may note the inherent strength of language, which like 'a mountain river' is always forcing its way out. We may witness the delight in imitation and repetition, and some of the laws by which sounds pass into one another. We may learn something also from the falterings of old age, the searching for words, and the confusion of them with one another, the forgetfulness of proper names (more commonly than of other words because they are more isolated), aphasia, and the like. There are philological lessons also to be gathered from nicknames, from provincialisms, from the slang of great cities, from the argot of Paris (that language of suffering and crime, so pathetically described by Victor Hugo), from the imperfect articulation of the deaf and dumb, from the jabbering of animals, from the analysis of sounds in relation to the organs of speech. The phonograph affords a visible evidence of the nature and divisions of sound; we may be truly said to know what we can manufacture. Artificial languages, such as that of Bishop Wilkins, are chiefly useful in showing what language is not. The study of any foreign language may be made also a study of Comparative Philology. There are several points, such as the nature of irregular verbs, of indeclinable parts of speech, the influence of euphony, the decay or loss of inflections, the elements of syntax, which may be examined as well in the history of our own language as of any other. A few well-selected questions may lead the student at once into the heart of the mystery: such as, Why are the pronouns and the verb of existence generally more irregular than any other parts of speech? Why is the number of words so small in which the sound is an echo of the sense? Why does the meaning of words depart so widely from their etymology? Why do substantives often differ in meaning from the verbs to which they are related, adverbs from adjectives? Why do words differing in origin coalesce in the same sound though retaining their differences of meaning? Why are some verbs impersonal? Why are there only so many parts of speech, and on what principle are they divided? These are a few crucial questions which give us an insight from different points of view into the true nature of language.

(6) Thus far we have been endeavouring to strip off from language the false appearances in which grammar and philology, or the love of system generally, have clothed it. We have also sought to indicate the sources of our knowledge of it and the spirit in which we should approach it, we may now proceed to consider some of the principles or natural laws which have created or modified it.

i. The first and simplest of all the principles of language, common also to the animals, is imitation. The lion roars, the wolf howls in the solitude of the forest: they are answered by similar cries heard from a distance. The bird, too, mimics the voice of man and makes answer to him. Man tells to man the secret place in which he is hiding himself; he remembers and repeats the sound which he has heard. The love of imitation becomes a passion and an instinct to him. Primitive men learnt to speak from one another, like a child from its mother or nurse. They learnt of course a rudimentary, half-articulate language, the cry or song or speech which was the expression of what we now call human thoughts and feelings. We may still remark how much greater and more natural the exercise of the power is in the use of language than in any other process or action of the human mind.

ii. Imitation provided the first material of language: but it was 'without form and void.' During how many years or hundreds or thousands of years the imitative or half-articulate stage continued there is no possibility of determining. But we may reasonably conjecture that there was a time when the vocal utterance of man was intermediate between what we now call language and the cry of a bird or animal. Speech before language was a rudis indigestaque materies, not yet distributed into words and sentences, in which the cry of fear or joy mingled with more definite sounds recognized by custom as the expressions of things or events. It was the principle of analogy which introduced into this 'indigesta moles' order and measure. It was Anaxagoras' omou panta chremata, eita nous elthon diekosmese: the light of reason lighted up all things and at once began to arrange them. In every sentence, in every word and every termination of a word, this power of forming relations to one another was contained. There was a proportion of sound to sound, of meaning to meaning, of meaning to sound. The cases and numbers of nouns, the persons, tenses, numbers of verbs, were generally on the same or nearly the same pattern and had the same meaning. The sounds by which they were expressed were rough-hewn at first; after a while they grew more refined--the natural laws of euphony began to affect them. The rules of syntax are likewise based upon analogy. Time has an analogy with space, arithmetic with geometry. Not only in musical notes, but in the quantity, quality, accent, rhythm of human speech, trivial or serious, there is a law of proportion. As in things of beauty, as in all nature, in the composition as well as in the motion of all things, there is a similarity of relations by which they are held together.

It would be a mistake to suppose that the analogies of language are always uniform: there may be often a choice between several, and sometimes one and sometimes another will prevail. In Greek there are three declensions of nouns; the forms of cases in one of them may intrude upon another. Similarly verbs in -omega and -mu iota interchange forms of tenses, and the completed paradigm of the verb is often made up of both. The same nouns may be partly declinable and partly indeclinable, and in some of their cases may have fallen out of use. Here are rules with exceptions; they are not however really exceptions, but contain in themselves indications of other rules. Many of these interruptions or variations of analogy occur in pronouns or in the verb of existence of which the forms were too common and therefore too deeply imbedded in language entirely to drop out. The same verbs in the same meaning may sometimes take one case, sometimes another. The participle may also have the character of an adjective, the adverb either of an adjective or of a preposition. These exceptions are as regular as the rules, but the causes of them are seldom known to us.

Language, like the animal and vegetable worlds, is everywhere intersected by the lines of analogy. Like number from which it seems to be derived, the principle of analogy opens the eyes of men to discern the similarities and differences of things, and their relations to one another. At first these are such as lie on the surface only; after a time they are seen by men to reach farther down into the nature of things. Gradually in language they arrange themselves into a sort of imperfect system; groups of personal and case endings are placed side by side. The fertility of language produces many more than are wanted; and the superfluous ones are utilized by the assignment to them of new meanings. The vacuity and the superfluity are thus partially compensated by each other. It must be remembered that in all the languages which have a literature, certainly in Sanskrit, Greek, Latin, we are not at the beginning but almost at the end of the linguistic process; we have reached a time when the verb and the noun are nearly perfected, though in no language did they completely perfect themselves, because for some unknown reason the motive powers of languages seem to have ceased when they were on the eve of completion: they became fixed or crystallized in an imperfect form either from the influence of writing and literature, or because no further differentiation of them was required for the intelligibility of language. So not without admixture and confusion and displacement and contamination of sounds and the meanings of words, a lower stage of language passes into a higher. Thus far we can see and no further. When we ask the reason why this principle of analogy prevails in all the vast domain of language, there is no answer to the question; or no other answer but this, that there are innumerable ways in which, like number, analogy permeates, not only language, but the whole world, both visible and intellectual. We know from experience that it does not (a) arise from any conscious act of reflection that the accusative of a Latin noun in 'us' should end in 'um;' nor (b) from any necessity of being understood,--much less articulation would suffice for this; nor (c) from greater convenience or expressiveness of particular sounds. Such notions were certainly far enough away from the mind of primitive man. We may speak of a latent instinct, of a survival of the fittest, easiest, most euphonic, most economical of breath, in the case of one of two competing sounds; but these expressions do not add anything to our knowledge. We may try to grasp the infinity of language either under the figure of a limitless plain divided into countries and districts by natural boundaries, or of a vast river eternally flowing whose origin is concealed from us; we may apprehend partially the laws by which speech is regulated: but we do not know, and we seem as if we should never know, any more than in the parallel case of the origin of species, how vocal sounds received life and grew, and in the form of languages came to be distributed over the earth.

iii. Next in order to analogy in the formation of language or even prior to it comes the principle of onomatopea, which is itself a kind of analogy or similarity of sound and meaning. In by far the greater number of words it has become disguised and has disappeared; but in no stage of language is it entirely lost. It belongs chiefly to early language, in which words were few; and its influence grew less and less as time went on. To the ear which had a sense of harmony it became a barbarism which disturbed the flow and equilibrium of discourse; it was an excrescence which had to be cut out, a survival which needed to be got rid of, because it was out of keeping with the rest. It remained for the most part only as a formative principle, which used words and letters not as crude imitations of other natural sounds, but as symbols of ideas which were naturally associated with them. It received in another way a new character; it affected not so much single words, as larger portions of human speech. It regulated the juxtaposition of sounds and the cadence of sentences. It was the music, not of song, but of speech, in prose as well as verse. The old onomatopea of primitive language was refined into an onomatopea of a higher kind, in which it is no longer true to say that a particular sound corresponds to a motion or action of man or beast or movement of nature, but that in all the higher uses of language the sound is the echo of the sense, especially in poetry, in which beauty and expressiveness are given to human thoughts by the harmonious composition of the words, syllables, letters, accents, quantities, rhythms, rhymes, varieties and contrasts of all sorts. The poet with his 'Break, break, break' or his e pasin nekuessi kataphthimenoisin anassein or his 'longius ex altoque sinum trahit,' can produce a far finer music than any crude imitations of things or actions in sound, although a letter or two having this imitative power may be a lesser element of beauty in such passages. The same subtle sensibility, which adapts the word to the thing, adapts the sentence or cadence to the general meaning or spirit of the passage. This is the higher onomatopea which has banished the cruder sort as unworthy to have a place in great languages and literatures.

We can see clearly enough that letters or collocations of letters do by various degrees of strength or weakness, length or shortness, emphasis or pitch, become the natural expressions of the finer parts of human feeling or thought. And not only so, but letters themselves have a significance; as Plato observes that the letter rho accent is expressive of motion, the letters delta and tau of binding and rest, the letter lambda of smoothness, nu of inwardness, the letter eta of length, the letter omicron of roundness. These were often combined so as to form composite notions, as for example in tromos (trembling), trachus (rugged), thrauein (crush), krouein (strike), thruptein (break), pumbein (whirl),--in all which words we notice a parallel composition of sounds in their English equivalents. Plato also remarks, as we remark, that the onomatopoetic principle is far from prevailing uniformly, and further that no explanation of language consistently corresponds with any system of philosophy, however great may be the light which language throws upon the nature of the mind. Both in Greek and English we find groups of words such as string, swing, sling, spring, sting, which are parallel to one another and may be said to derive their vocal effect partly from contrast of letters, but in which it is impossible to assign a precise amount of meaning to each of the expressive and onomatopoetic letters. A few of them are directly imitative, as for example the omega in oon, which represents the round form of the egg by the figure of the mouth: or bronte (thunder), in which the fulness of the sound of the word corresponds to the thing signified by it; or bombos (buzzing), of which the first syllable, as in its English equivalent, has the meaning of a deep sound. We may observe also (as we see in the case of the poor stammerer) that speech has the co-operation of the whole body and may be often assisted or half expressed by gesticulation. A sound or word is not the work of the vocal organs only; nearly the whole of the upper part of the human frame, including head, chest, lungs, have a share in creating it; and it may be accompanied by a movement of the eyes, nose, fingers, hands, feet which contributes to the effect of it.

The principle of onomatopea has fallen into discredit, partly because it has been supposed to imply an actual manufacture of words out of syllables and letters, like a piece of joiner's work,--a theory of language which is more and more refuted by facts, and more and more going out of fashion with philologians; and partly also because the traces of onomatopea in separate words become almost obliterated in the course of ages. The poet of language cannot put in and pull out letters, as a painter might insert or blot out a shade of colour to give effect to his picture. It would be ridiculous for him to alter any received form of a word in order to render it more expressive of the sense. He can only select, perhaps out of some dialect, the form which is already best adapted to his purpose. The true onomatopea is not a creative, but a formative principle, which in the later stage of the history of language ceases to act upon individual words; but still works through the collocation of them in the sentence or paragraph, and the adaptation of every word, syllable, letter to one another and to the rhythm of the whole passage.

iv. Next, under a distinct head, although not separable from the preceding, may be considered the differentiation of languages, i.e. the manner in which differences of meaning and form have arisen in them. Into their first creation we have ceased to enquire: it is their aftergrowth with which we are now concerned. How did the roots or substantial portions of words become modified or inflected? and how did they receive separate meanings? First we remark that words are attracted by the sounds and senses of other words, so that they form groups of nouns and verbs analogous in sound and sense to one another, each noun or verb putting forth inflexions, generally of two or three patterns, and with exceptions. We do not say that we know how sense became first allied to sound; but we have no difficulty in ascertaining how the sounds and meanings of words were in time parted off or differentiated. (1) The chief causes which regulate the variations of sound are (a) double or differing analogies, which lead sometimes to one form, sometimes to another (b) euphony, by which is meant chiefly the greater pleasure to the ear and the greater facility to the organs of speech which is given by a new formation or pronunciation of a word (c) the necessity of finding new expressions for new classes or processes of things. We are told that changes of sound take place by innumerable gradations until a whole tribe or community or society find themselves acquiescing in a new pronunciation or use of language. Yet no one observes the change, or is at all aware that in the course of a lifetime he and his contemporaries have appreciably varied their intonation or use of words. On the other hand, the necessities of language seem to require that the intermediate sounds or meanings of words should quickly become fixed or set and not continue in a state of transition. The process of settling down is aided by the organs of speech and by the use of writing and printing. (2) The meaning of words varies because ideas vary or the number of things which is included under them or with which they are associated is increased. A single word is thus made to do duty for many more things than were formerly expressed by it; and it parts into different senses when the classes of things or ideas which are represented by it are themselves different and distinct. A figurative use of a word may easily pass into a new sense: a new meaning caught up by association may become more important than all the rest. The good or neutral sense of a word, such as Jesuit, Puritan, Methodist, Heretic, has been often converted into a bad one by the malevolence of party spirit. Double forms suggest different meanings and are often used to express them; and the form or accent of a word has been not unfrequently altered when there is a difference of meaning. The difference of gender in nouns is utilized for the same reason. New meanings of words push themselves into the vacant spaces of language and retire when they are no longer needed. Language equally abhors vacancy and superfluity. But the remedial measures by which both are eliminated are not due to any conscious action of the human mind; nor is the force exerted by them constraining or necessary.

(7) We have shown that language, although subject to laws, is far from being of an exact and uniform nature. We may now speak briefly of the faults of language. They may be compared to the faults of Geology, in which different strata cross one another or meet at an angle, or mix with one another either by slow transitions or by violent convulsions, leaving many lacunae which can be no longer filled up, and often becoming so complex that no true explanation of them can be given. So in language there are the cross influences of meaning and sound, of logic and grammar, of differing analogies, of words and the inflexions of words, which often come into conflict with each other. The grammarian, if he were to form new words, would make them all of the same pattern according to what he conceives to be the rule, that is, the more common usage of language. The subtlety of nature goes far beyond art, and it is complicated by irregularity, so that often we can hardly say that there is a right or wrong in the formation of words. For almost any formation which is not at variance with the first principles of language is possible and may be defended.

The imperfection of language is really due to the formation and correlation of words by accident, that is to say, by principles which are unknown to us. Hence we see why Plato, like ourselves unable to comprehend the whole of language, was constrained to 'supplement the poor creature imitation by another poor creature convention.' But the poor creature convention in the end proves too much for all the rest: for we do not ask what is the origin of words or whether they are formed according to a correct analogy, but what is the usage of them; and we are compelled to admit with Hermogenes in Plato and with Horace that usage is the ruling principle, 'quem penes arbitrium est, et jus et norma loquendi.'

(8) There are two ways in which a language may attain permanence or fixity. First, it may have been embodied in poems or hymns or laws, which may be repeated for hundreds, perhaps for thousands of years with a religious accuracy, so that to the priests or rhapsodists of a nation the whole or the greater part of a language is literally preserved; secondly, it may be written down and in a written form distributed more or less widely among the whole nation. In either case the language which is familiarly spoken may have grown up wholly or in a great measure independently of them. (1) The first of these processes has been sometimes attended by the result that the sound of the words has been carefully preserved and that the meaning of them has either perished wholly, or is only doubtfully recovered by the efforts of modern philology. The verses have been repeated as a chant or part of a ritual, but they

have had no relation to ordinary life or speech. (2) The invention of writing again is commonly attributed to a particular epoch, and we are apt to think that such an inestimable gift would have immediately been diffused over a whole country. But it may have taken a long time to perfect the art of writing, and another long period may have elapsed before it came into common use. Its influence on language has been increased ten, twenty or one hundred fold by the invention of printing.

Before the growth of poetry or the invention of writing, languages were only dialects. So they continued to be in parts of the country in which writing was not used or in which there was no diffusion of literature. In most of the counties of England there is still a provincial style, which has been sometimes made by a great poet the vehicle of his fancies. When a book sinks into the mind of a nation, such as Luther's Bible or the Authorized English Translation of the Bible, or again great classical works like Shakspere or Milton, not only have new powers of expression been diffused through a whole nation, but a great step towards uniformity has been made. The instinct of language demands regular grammar and correct spelling: these are imprinted deeply on the tablets of a nation's memory by a common use of classical and popular writers. In our own day we have attained to a point at which nearly every printed book is spelt correctly and written grammatically.

(9) Proceeding further to trace the influence of literature on language we note some other causes which have affected the higher use of it: such as (1) the necessity of clearness and connexion; (2) the fear of tautology; (3) the influence of metre, rhythm, rhyme, and of the language of prose and verse upon one another; (4) the power of idiom and quotation; (5) the relativeness of words to one another.

It has been usual to depreciate modern languages when compared with ancient. The latter are regarded as furnishing a type of excellence to which the former cannot attain. But the truth seems to be that modern languages, if through the loss of inflections and genders they lack some power or beauty or expressiveness or precision which is possessed by the ancient, are in many other respects superior to them: the thought is generally clearer, the connexion closer, the sentence and paragraph are better distributed. The best modern languages, for example English or French, possess as great a power of self-improvement as the Latin, if not as the Greek. Nor does there seem to be any reason why they should ever decline or decay. It is a popular remark that our great writers are beginning to disappear: it may also be remarked that whenever a great writer appears in the future he will find the English language as perfect and as ready for use as in the days of Shakspere or Milton. There is no reason to suppose that English or French will ever be reduced to the low level of Modern Greek or of Mediaeval Latin. The wide diffusion of great authors would make such a decline impossible. Nor will modern languages be easily broken up by amalgamation with each other. The distance between them is too wide to be spanned, the differences are too great to be overcome, and the use of printing makes it impossible that one of them should ever be lost in another.

The structure of the English language differs greatly from that of either Latin or Greek. In the two latter, especially in Greek, sentences are joined together by connecting particles. They are distributed on the right hand and on the left by men, de, alla, kaitoi, kai de and the like, or deduced from one another by ara, de, oun, toinun and the like. In English the majority of sentences are independent and in apposition to one another; they are laid side by side or slightly connected by the copula. But within the sentence the expression of the logical relations of the clauses is closer and more exact: there is less of apposition and participial structure. The sentences thus laid side by side are also constructed into paragraphs; these again are less distinctly marked in Greek and Latin than in English. Generally French, German, and English have an advantage over the classical languages in point of accuracy. The three concords are more accurately observed in English than in either Greek or Latin. On the other hand, the extension of the familiar use of the masculine and feminine gender to objects of sense and abstract ideas as well as to men and animals no doubt lends a nameless grace to style which we have a difficulty in appreciating, and the possible variety in the order of words gives more flexibility and also a kind of dignity to the period. Of the comparative effect of accent and quantity and of the relation between them in ancient and modern languages we are not able to judge.

Another quality in which modern are superior to ancient languages is freedom from tautology. No English style is thought tolerable in which, except for the sake of emphasis, the same words are repeated at short intervals. Of course the length of the interval must depend on the character of the word. Striking words and expressions cannot be allowed to reappear, if at all, except at the distance of a page or more. Pronouns, prepositions, conjunctions may or rather must recur in successive lines. It seems to be a kind of impertinence to the reader and strikes unpleasantly both on the mind and on the ear that the same sounds should be used twice over, when another word or turn of expression would have given a new shade of meaning to the thought and would have added a pleasing variety to the sound. And the mind equally rejects the repetition of the word and the use of a mere synonym for it,-- e.g. felicity and happiness. The cultivated mind desires something more, which a skilful writer is easily able to supply out of his treasure-house.

The fear of tautology has doubtless led to the multiplications of words and the meanings of words, and generally to an enlargement of the vocabulary. It is a very early instinct of language; for ancient poetry is almost as free from tautology as the best modern writings. The speech of young children, except in so far as they are compelled to repeat themselves by the fewness of their words, also escapes from it. When they grow up and have ideas which are beyond their powers of expression, especially in writing, tautology begins to appear. In like manner when language is 'contaminated' by philosophy it is apt to become awkward, to stammer and repeat itself, to lose its flow and freedom. No philosophical writer with the exception of Plato, who is himself not free from tautology, and perhaps Bacon, has attained to any high degree of literary excellence.

To poetry the form and polish of language is chiefly to be attributed; and the most critical period in the history of language is the transition from verse to prose. At first mankind were contented to express their thoughts in a set form of words having a kind of rhythm; to which regularity was given by accent and quantity. But after a time they demanded a greater degree of freedom, and to those who had all their life been hearing poetry the first introduction of prose had the charm of novelty. The prose romances into which the Homeric Poems were converted, for a while probably gave more delight to the hearers or readers of them than the Poems themselves, and in time the relation of the two was reversed: the poems which had once been a necessity of the human mind became a luxury: they were now superseded by prose, which in all succeeding ages became the natural vehicle of expression to all mankind. Henceforward prose and poetry formed each other. A comparatively slender link between them was also furnished by proverbs. We may trace in poetry how the simple succession of lines, not without monotony, has passed into a complicated period, and how in prose, rhythm and accent and the order of words and the balance of clauses, sometimes not without a slight admixture of rhyme, make up a new kind of harmony, swelling into strains not less majestic than those of Homer, Virgil, or Dante.

One of the most curious and characteristic features of language, affecting both syntax and style, is idiom. The meaning of the word 'idiom' is that which is peculiar, that which is familiar, the word or expression which strikes us or comes home to us, which is more readily understood or more easily remembered. It is a quality which really exists in infinite degrees, which we turn into differences of kind by applying the term only to conspicuous and striking examples of words or phrases which have this quality. It often supersedes the laws of language or the rules of grammar, or rather is to be regarded as another law of language which is natural and necessary. The word or phrase which has been repeated many times over is more intelligible and familiar to us than one which is rare, and our familiarity with it more than compensates for incorrectness or inaccuracy in the use of it. Striking expressions also which have moved the hearts of nations or are the precious stones and jewels of great authors partake of the nature of idioms: they are taken out of the sphere of grammar and are exempt from the proprieties of language. Every one knows that we often put words together in a manner which would be intolerable if it were not idiomatic. We cannot argue either about the meaning of words or the use of constructions that because they are used in one connexion they will be legitimate in another, unless we allow for this principle. We can bear to have words and sentences used in new senses or in a new order or even a little perverted in meaning when we are quite familiar with them. Quotations are as often applied in a sense which the author did not intend as in that which he did. The parody of the words of Shakspere or of the Bible, which has in it something of the nature of a lie, is far from unpleasing to us. The better known words, even if their meaning be perverted, are more agreeable to us and have a greater power over us. Most of us have experienced a sort of delight and feeling of curiosity when we first came across or when we first used for ourselves a new word or phrase or figure of speech.

There are associations of sound and of sense by which every word is linked to every other. One letter harmonizes with another; every verb or noun derives its meaning, not only from itself, but from the words with which it is associated. Some reflection of them near or distant is embodied in it. In any new use of a word all the existing uses of it have to be considered. Upon these depends the question whether it will bear the proposed extension of meaning or not. According to the famous expression of Luther, 'Words are living creatures, having hands and feet.' When they cease to retain this living power of adaptation, when they are only put together like the parts of a piece of furniture, language becomes unpoetical, in expressive, dead.

Grammars would lead us to suppose that words have a fixed form and sound. Lexicons assign to each word a definite meaning or meanings. They both tend to obscure the fact that the sentence precedes the word and that all language is relative. (1) It is relative to its own context. Its meaning is modified by what has been said before and after in the same or in some other passage: without comparing the context we are not sure whether it is used in the same sense even in two successive sentences. (2) It is relative to facts, to time, place, and occasion: when they are already known to the hearer or reader, they may be presupposed; there is no need to allude to them further. (3) It is relative to the knowledge of the writer and reader or of the speaker and hearer. Except for the sake of order and consecutiveness nothing ought to be expressed which is already commonly or universally known. A word or two may be sufficient to give an intimation to a friend; a long or elaborate speech or composition is required to explain some new idea to a popular audience or to the ordinary reader or to a young pupil. Grammars and dictionaries are not to be despised; for in teaching we need clearness rather than subtlety. But we must not therefore forget that there is also a higher ideal of language in which all is relative--sounds to sounds, words to words, the parts to the whole--in which besides the lesser context of the book or speech, there is also the larger context of history and circumstances.

The study of Comparative Philology has introduced into the world a new science which more than any other binds up man with nature, and distant ages and countries with one another. It may be said to have thrown a light upon all other sciences and upon the nature of the human mind itself. The true conception of it dispels many errors, not only of metaphysics and theology, but also of natural knowledge. Yet it is far from certain that this newly-found science will continue to progress in the same surprising manner as heretofore; or that even if our materials are largely increased, we shall arrive at much more definite conclusions than at present. Like some other branches of knowledge, it may be approaching a point at which it can no longer be profitably studied. But at any rate it has brought back the philosophy of language from theory to fact; it has passed out of the region of guesses and hypotheses, and has attained the dignity of an Inductive Science. And it is not without practical and political importance. It gives a new interest to distant and subject countries; it brings back the dawning light from one end of the earth to the other. Nations, like individuals, are better understood by us when we know something of their early life; and when they are better understood by us, we feel more kindly towards them. Lastly, we may remember that all knowledge is valuable for its own sake; and we may also hope that a deeper insight into the nature of human speech will give us a greater command of it and enable us to make a nobler use of it. (Compare again W. Humboldt, 'Ueber die Verschiedenheit des menschlichen Sprachbaues;' M. Muller, 'Lectures on the Science of Language;' Steinthal, 'Einleitung in die Psychologie und Sprachwissenschaft:' and for the latter part of the Essay, Delbruck, 'Study of Language;' Paul's 'Principles of the History of Language:' to the latter work the author of this Essay is largely indebted.)

CRATYLUS

By Plato

Translated by Benjamin Jowett

PERSONS OF THE DIALOGUE:
Socrates,
Hermogenes,
Cratylus.

HERMOGENES
Suppose that we make Socrates a party to the argument?

CRATYLUS
If you please.

HERMOGENES
I should explain to you, Socrates, that our friend Cratylus has been arguing about names; he says that they are natural and not conventional; not a portion of the human voice which men agree to use; but that there is a truth or correctness in them, which is the same for Hellenes as for barbarians. Whereupon I ask him, whether his own name of Cratylus is a true name or not, and he answers 'Yes.' And Socrates? 'Yes.' Then every man's name, as I tell him, is that which he is called. To this he replies--'If all the world were to call you Hermogenes, that would not be your name.' And when I am anxious to have a further explanation he is ironical and mysterious, and seems to imply that he has a notion of his own about the matter, if he would only tell, and could entirely convince me, if he chose to be intelligible. Tell me, Socrates, what this oracle means; or rather tell me, if you will be so good, what is your own view of the truth or correctness of names, which I would far sooner hear.

SOCRATES

Son of Hipponicus, there is an ancient saying, that 'hard is the knowledge of the good.' And the knowledge of names is a great part of knowledge. If I had not been poor, I might have heard the fifty-drachma course of the great Prodicus, which is a complete education in grammar and language--these are his own words--and then I should have been at once able to answer your question about the correctness of names. But, indeed, I have only heard the single-drachma course, and therefore, I do not know the truth about such matters; I will, however, gladly assist you and Cratylus in the investigation of them. When he declares that your name is not really Hermogenes, I suspect that he is only making fun of you;--he means to say that you are no true son of Hermes, because you are always looking after a fortune and never in luck. But, as I was saying, there is a good deal of difficulty in this sort of knowledge, and therefore we had better leave the question open until we have heard both sides.

HERMOGENES

I have often talked over this matter, both with Cratylus and others, and cannot convince myself that there is any principle of correctness in names other than convention and agreement; any name which you give, in my opinion, is the right one, and if you change that and give another, the new name is as correct as the old--we frequently change the names of our slaves, and the newly-imposed name is as good as the old: for there is no name given to anything by nature; all is convention and habit of the users;--such is my view. But if I am mistaken I shall be happy to hear and learn of Cratylus, or of any one else.

SOCRATES

I dare say that you may be right, Hermogenes: let us see;--Your meaning is, that the name of each thing is only that which anybody agrees to call it?

HERMOGENES

That is my notion.

SOCRATES

Whether the giver of the name be an individual or a city?

HERMOGENES

Yes.

SOCRATES

Well, now, let me take an instance;--suppose that I call a man a horse or a horse a man, you mean to say that a man will be rightly called a horse by me individually, and rightly called a man by the rest of the world; and a horse again would be rightly called a man by me and a horse by the world:--that is your meaning?

HERMOGENES

He would, according to my view.

SOCRATES

But how about truth, then? you would acknowledge that there is in words a true and a false?

HERMOGENES

Certainly.

SOCRATES
And there are true and false propositions?

HERMOGENES
To be sure.

SOCRATES
And a true proposition says that which is, and a false proposition says that which is not?

HERMOGENES
Yes; what other answer is possible?

SOCRATES
Then in a proposition there is a true and false?

HERMOGENES
Certainly.

SOCRATES
But is a proposition true as a whole only, and are the parts untrue?

HERMOGENES
No; the parts are true as well as the whole.

SOCRATES
Would you say the large parts and not the smaller ones, or every part?

HERMOGENES
I should say that every part is true.

SOCRATES
Is a proposition resolvable into any part smaller than a name?

HERMOGENES
No; that is the smallest.

SOCRATES
Then the name is a part of the true proposition?

HERMOGENES
Yes.

SOCRATES
Yes, and a true part, as you say.

HERMOGENES
Yes.

SOCRATES

And is not the part of a falsehood also a falsehood?

HERMOGENES

Yes.

SOCRATES

Then, if propositions may be true and false, names may be true and false?

HERMOGENES

So we must infer.

SOCRATES

And the name of anything is that which any one affirms to be the name?

HERMOGENES

Yes.

SOCRATES

And will there be so many names of each thing as everybody says that there are? and will they be true names at the time of uttering them?

HERMOGENES

Yes, Socrates, I can conceive no correctness of names other than this; you give one name, and I another; and in different cities and countries there are different names for the same things; Hellenes differ from barbarians in their use of names, and the several Hellenic tribes from one another.

SOCRATES

But would you say, Hermogenes, that the things differ as the names differ? and are they relative to individuals, as Protagoras tells us? For he says that man is the measure of all things, and that things are to me as they appear to me, and that they are to you as they appear to you. Do you agree with him, or would you say that things have a permanent essence of their own?

HERMOGENES

There have been times, Socrates, when I have been driven in my perplexity to take refuge with Protagoras; not that I agree with him at all.

SOCRATES

What! have you ever been driven to admit that there was no such thing as a bad man?

HERMOGENES

No, indeed; but I have often had reason to think that there are very bad men, and a good many of them.

SOCRATES

Well, and have you ever found any very good ones?

HERMOGENES

Not many.

SOCRATES
Still you have found them?

HERMOGENES
Yes.

SOCRATES
And would you hold that the very good were the very wise, and the very evil very foolish? Would that be your view?

HERMOGENES
It would.

SOCRATES
But if Protagoras is right, and the truth is that things are as they appear to any one, how can some of us be wise and some of us foolish?

HERMOGENES
Impossible.

SOCRATES
And if, on the other hand, wisdom and folly are really distinguishable, you will allow, I think, that the assertion of Protagoras can hardly be correct. For if what appears to each man is true to him, one man cannot in reality be wiser than another.

HERMOGENES
He cannot.

SOCRATES
Nor will you be disposed to say with Euthydemus, that all things equally belong to all men at the same moment and always; for neither on his view can there be some good and others bad, if virtue and vice are always equally to be attributed to all.

HERMOGENES
There cannot.

SOCRATES
But if neither is right, and things are not relative to individuals, and all things do not equally belong to all at the same moment and always, they must be supposed to have their own proper and permanent essence: they are not in relation to us, or influenced by us, fluctuating according to our fancy, but they are independent, and maintain to their own essence the relation prescribed by nature.

HERMOGENES
I think, Socrates, that you have said the truth.

SOCRATES

Does what I am saying apply only to the things themselves, or equally to the actions which proceed from them? Are not actions also a class of being?

HERMOGENES
Yes, the actions are real as well as the things.

SOCRATES
Then the actions also are done according to their proper nature, and not according to our opinion of them? In cutting, for example, we do not cut as we please, and with any chance instrument; but we cut with the proper instrument only, and according to the natural process of cutting; and the natural process is right and will succeed, but any other will fail and be of no use at all.

HERMOGENES
I should say that the natural way is the right way.

SOCRATES
Again, in burning, not every way is the right way; but the right way is the natural way, and the right instrument the natural instrument.

HERMOGENES
True.

SOCRATES
And this holds good of all actions?

HERMOGENES
Yes.

SOCRATES
And speech is a kind of action?

HERMOGENES
True.

SOCRATES
And will a man speak correctly who speaks as he pleases? Will not the successful speaker rather be he who speaks in the natural way of speaking, and as things ought to be spoken, and with the natural instrument? Any other mode of speaking will result in error and failure.

HERMOGENES
I quite agree with you.

SOCRATES
And is not naming a part of speaking? for in giving names men speak.

HERMOGENES
That is true.

SOCRATES
And if speaking is a sort of action and has a relation to acts, is not naming also a sort of action?

HERMOGENES
True.

SOCRATES
And we saw that actions were not relative to ourselves, but had a special nature of their own?

HERMOGENES
Precisely.

SOCRATES
Then the argument would lead us to infer that names ought to be given according to a natural process, and with a proper instrument, and not at our pleasure: in this and no other way shall we name with success.

HERMOGENES
I agree.

SOCRATES
But again, that which has to be cut has to be cut with something?

HERMOGENES
Yes.

SOCRATES
And that which has to be woven or pierced has to be woven or pierced with something?

HERMOGENES
Certainly.

SOCRATES
And that which has to be named has to be named with something?

HERMOGENES
True.

SOCRATES
What is that with which we pierce?

HERMOGENES
An awl.

SOCRATES
And with which we weave?

HERMOGENES

A shuttle.

SOCRATES
And with which we name?

HERMOGENES
A name.

SOCRATES
Very good: then a name is an instrument?

HERMOGENES
Certainly.

SOCRATES
Suppose that I ask, 'What sort of instrument is a shuttle?' And you answer, 'A weaving instrument.'

HERMOGENES
Well.

SOCRATES
And I ask again, 'What do we do when we weave?'--The answer is, that we separate or disengage the warp from the woof.

HERMOGENES
Very true.

SOCRATES
And may not a similar description be given of an awl, and of instruments in general?

HERMOGENES
To be sure.

SOCRATES
And now suppose that I ask a similar question about names: will you answer me? Regarding the name as an instrument, what do we do when we name?

HERMOGENES
I cannot say.

SOCRATES
Do we not give information to one another, and distinguish things according to their natures?

HERMOGENES
Certainly we do.

SOCRATES

Then a name is an instrument of teaching and of distinguishing natures, as the shuttle is of distinguishing the threads of the web.

HERMOGENES
Yes.

SOCRATES
And the shuttle is the instrument of the weaver?

HERMOGENES
Assuredly.

SOCRATES
Then the weaver will use the shuttle well--and well means like a weaver? and the teacher will use the name well--and well means like a teacher?

HERMOGENES
Yes.

SOCRATES
And when the weaver uses the shuttle, whose work will he be using well?

HERMOGENES
That of the carpenter.

SOCRATES
And is every man a carpenter, or the skilled only?

HERMOGENES
Only the skilled.

SOCRATES
And when the piercer uses the awl, whose work will he be using well?

HERMOGENES
That of the smith.

SOCRATES
And is every man a smith, or only the skilled?

HERMOGENES
The skilled only.

SOCRATES
And when the teacher uses the name, whose work will he be using?

HERMOGENES
There again I am puzzled.

SOCRATES

Cannot you at least say who gives us the names which we use?

HERMOGENES

Indeed I cannot.

SOCRATES

Does not the law seem to you to give us them?

HERMOGENES

Yes, I suppose so.

SOCRATES

Then the teacher, when he gives us a name, uses the work of the legislator?

HERMOGENES

I agree.

SOCRATES

And is every man a legislator, or the skilled only?

HERMOGENES

The skilled only.

SOCRATES

Then, Hermogenes, not every man is able to give a name, but only a maker of names; and this is the legislator, who of all skilled artisans in the world is the rarest.

HERMOGENES

True.

SOCRATES

And how does the legislator make names? and to what does he look? Consider this in the light of the previous instances: to what does the carpenter look in making the shuttle? Does he not look to that which is naturally fitted to act as a shuttle?

HERMOGENES

Certainly.

SOCRATES

And suppose the shuttle to be broken in making, will he make another, looking to the broken one? or will he look to the form according to which he made the other?

HERMOGENES

To the latter, I should imagine.

SOCRATES

Might not that be justly called the true or ideal shuttle?

HERMOGENES
I think so.

SOCRATES
And whatever shuttles are wanted, for the manufacture of garments, thin or thick, of flaxen, woollen, or other material, ought all of them to have the true form of the shuttle; and whatever is the shuttle best adapted to each kind of work, that ought to be the form which the maker produces in each case.

HERMOGENES
Yes.

SOCRATES
And the same holds of other instruments: when a man has discovered the instrument which is naturally adapted to each work, he must express this natural form, and not others which he fancies, in the material, whatever it may be, which he employs; for example, he ought to know how to put into iron the forms of awls adapted by nature to their several uses?

HERMOGENES
Certainly.

SOCRATES
And how to put into wood forms of shuttles adapted by nature to their uses?

HERMOGENES
True.

SOCRATES
For the several forms of shuttles naturally answer to the several kinds of webs; and this is true of instruments in general.

HERMOGENES
Yes.

SOCRATES
Then, as to names: ought not our legislator also to know how to put the true natural name of each thing into sounds and syllables, and to make and give all names with a view to the ideal name, if he is to be a namer in any true sense? And we must remember that different legislators will not use the same syllables. For neither does every smith, although he may be making the same instrument for the same purpose, make them all of the same iron. The form must be the same, but the material may vary, and still the instrument may be equally good of whatever iron made, whether in Hellas or in a foreign country;--there is no difference.

HERMOGENES
Very true.

SOCRATES

And the legislator, whether he be Hellene or barbarian, is not therefore to be deemed by you a worse legislator, provided he gives the true and proper form of the name in whatever syllables; this or that country makes no matter.

HERMOGENES
Quite true.

SOCRATES
But who then is to determine whether the proper form is given to the shuttle, whatever sort of wood may be used? the carpenter who makes, or the weaver who is to use them?

HERMOGENES
I should say, he who is to use them, Socrates.

SOCRATES
And who uses the work of the lyre-maker? Will not he be the man who knows how to direct what is being done, and who will know also whether the work is being well done or not?

HERMOGENES
Certainly.

SOCRATES
And who is he?

HERMOGENES
The player of the lyre.

SOCRATES
And who will direct the shipwright?

HERMOGENES
The pilot.

SOCRATES
And who will be best able to direct the legislator in his work, and will know whether the work is well done, in this or any other country? Will not the user be the man?

HERMOGENES
Yes.

SOCRATES
And this is he who knows how to ask questions?

HERMOGENES
Yes.

SOCRATES
And how to answer them?

HERMOGENES

Yes.

SOCRATES

And him who knows how to ask and answer you would call a dialectician?

HERMOGENES

Yes; that would be his name.

SOCRATES

Then the work of the carpenter is to make a rudder, and the pilot has to direct him, if the rudder is to be well made.

HERMOGENES

True.

SOCRATES

And the work of the legislator is to give names, and the dialectician must be his director if the names are to be rightly given?

HERMOGENES

That is true.

SOCRATES

Then, Hermogenes, I should say that this giving of names can be no such light matter as you fancy, or the work of light or chance persons; and Cratylus is right in saying that things have names by nature, and that not every man is an artificer of names, but he only who looks to the name which each thing by nature has, and is able to express the true forms of things in letters and syllables.

HERMOGENES

I cannot answer you, Socrates; but I find a difficulty in changing my opinion all in a moment, and I think that I should be more readily persuaded, if you would show me what this is which you term the natural fitness of names.

SOCRATES

My good Hermogenes, I have none to show. Was I not telling you just now (but you have forgotten), that I knew nothing, and proposing to share the enquiry with you? But now that you and I have talked over the matter, a step has been gained; for we have discovered that names have by nature a truth, and that not every man knows how to give a thing a name.

HERMOGENES

Very good.

SOCRATES

And what is the nature of this truth or correctness of names? That, if you care to know, is the next question.

HERMOGENES
Certainly, I care to know.

SOCRATES
Then reflect.

HERMOGENES
How shall I reflect?

SOCRATES
The true way is to have the assistance of those who know, and you must pay them well both in money and in thanks; these are the Sophists, of whom your brother, Callias, has--rather dearly--bought the reputation of wisdom. But you have not yet come into your inheritance, and therefore you had better go to him, and beg and entreat him to tell you what he has learnt from Protagoras about the fitness of names.

HERMOGENES
But how inconsistent should I be, if, whilst repudiating Protagoras and his truth ('Truth' was the title of the book of Protagoras; compare Theaet.), I were to attach any value to what he and his book affirm!

SOCRATES
Then if you despise him, you must learn of Homer and the poets.

HERMOGENES
And where does Homer say anything about names, and what does he say?

SOCRATES
He often speaks of them; notably and nobly in the places where he distinguishes the different names which Gods and men give to the same things. Does he not in these passages make a remarkable statement about the correctness of names? For the Gods must clearly be supposed to call things by their right and natural names; do you not think so?

HERMOGENES
Why, of course they call them rightly, if they call them at all. But to what are you referring?

SOCRATES
Do you not know what he says about the river in Troy who had a single combat with Hephaestus?

'Whom,' as he says, 'the Gods call Xanthus, and men call Scamander.'

HERMOGENES
I remember.

SOCRATES
Well, and about this river--to know that he ought to be called Xanthus and not Scamander--is not that a solemn lesson? Or about the bird which, as he says,

'The Gods call Chalcis, and men Cymindis:'

to be taught how much more correct the name Chalcis is than the name Cymindis--do you deem that a light matter? Or about Batieia and Myrina? (Compare Il. 'The hill which men call Batieia and the immortals the tomb of the sportive Myrina.') And there are many other observations of the same kind in Homer and other poets. Now, I think that this is beyond the understanding of you and me; but the names of Scamandrius and Astyanax, which he affirms to have been the names of Hector's son, are more within the range of human faculties, as I am disposed to think; and what the poet means by correctness may be more readily apprehended in that instance: you will remember I dare say the lines to which I refer? (Il.)

HERMOGENES
I do.

SOCRATES
Let me ask you, then, which did Homer think the more correct of the names given to Hector's son-- Astyanax or Scamandrius?

HERMOGENES
I do not know.

SOCRATES
How would you answer, if you were asked whether the wise or the unwise are more likely to give correct names?

HERMOGENES
I should say the wise, of course.

SOCRATES
And are the men or the women of a city, taken as a class, the wiser?

HERMOGENES
I should say, the men.

SOCRATES
And Homer, as you know, says that the Trojan men called him Astyanax (king of the city); but if the men called him Astyanax, the other name of Scamandrius could only have been given to him by the women.

HERMOGENES
That may be inferred.

SOCRATES
And must not Homer have imagined the Trojans to be wiser than their wives?

HERMOGENES
To be sure.

SOCRATES
Then he must have thought Astyanax to be a more correct name for the boy than Scamandrius?

HERMOGENES

Clearly.

SOCRATES

And what is the reason of this? Let us consider:--does he not himself suggest a very good reason, when he says,

'For he alone defended their city and long walls'?

This appears to be a good reason for calling the son of the saviour king of the city which his father was saving, as Homer observes.

HERMOGENES

I see.

SOCRATES

Why, Hermogenes, I do not as yet see myself; and do you?

HERMOGENES

No, indeed; not I.

SOCRATES

But tell me, friend, did not Homer himself also give Hector his name?

HERMOGENES

What of that?

SOCRATES

The name appears to me to be very nearly the same as the name of Astyanax--both are Hellenic; and a king (anax) and a holder (ektor) have nearly the same meaning, and are both descriptive of a king; for a man is clearly the holder of that of which he is king; he rules, and owns, and holds it. But, perhaps, you may think that I am talking nonsense; and indeed I believe that I myself did not know what I meant when I imagined that I had found some indication of the opinion of Homer about the correctness of names.

HERMOGENES

I assure you that I think otherwise, and I believe you to be on the right track.

SOCRATES

There is reason, I think, in calling the lion's whelp a lion, and the foal of a horse a horse; I am speaking only of the ordinary course of nature, when an animal produces after his kind, and not of extraordinary births;--if contrary to nature a horse have a calf, then I should not call that a foal but a calf; nor do I call any inhuman birth a man, but only a natural birth. And the same may be said of trees and other things. Do you agree with me?

HERMOGENES

Yes, I agree.

SOCRATES

Very good. But you had better watch me and see that I do not play tricks with you. For on the same principle the son of a king is to be called a king. And whether the syllables of the name are the same or not the same, makes no difference, provided the meaning is retained; nor does the addition or subtraction of a letter make any difference so long as the essence of the thing remains in possession of the name and appears in it.

HERMOGENES

What do you mean?

SOCRATES

A very simple matter. I may illustrate my meaning by the names of letters, which you know are not the same as the letters themselves with the exception of the four epsilon, upsilon, omicron, omega; the names of the rest, whether vowels or consonants, are made up of other letters which we add to them; but so long as we introduce the meaning, and there can be no mistake, the name of the letter is quite correct. Take, for example, the letter beta--the addition of eta, tau, alpha, gives no offence, and does not prevent the whole name from having the value which the legislator intended--so well did he know how to give the letters names.

HERMOGENES

I believe you are right.

SOCRATES

And may not the same be said of a king? a king will often be the son of a king, the good son or the noble son of a good or noble sire; and similarly the offspring of every kind, in the regular course of nature, is like the parent, and therefore has the same name. Yet the syllables may be disguised until they appear different to the ignorant person, and he may not recognize them, although they are the same, just as any one of us would not recognize the same drugs under different disguises of colour and smell, although to the physician, who regards the power of them, they are the same, and he is not put out by the addition; and in like manner the etymologist is not put out by the addition or transposition or subtraction of a letter or two, or indeed by the change of all the letters, for this need not interfere with the meaning. As was just now said, the names of Hector and Astyanax have only one letter alike, which is tau, and yet they have the same meaning. And how little in common with the letters of their names has Archepolis (ruler of the city)--and yet the meaning is the same. And there are many other names which just mean 'king.' Again, there are several names for a general, as, for example, Agis (leader) and Polemarchus (chief in war) and Eupolemus (good warrior); and others which denote a physician, as Iatrocles (famous healer) and Acesimbrotus (curer of mortals); and there are many others which might be cited, differing in their syllables and letters, but having the same meaning. Would you not say so?

HERMOGENES

Yes.

SOCRATES

The same names, then, ought to be assigned to those who follow in the course of nature?

HERMOGENES

Yes.

SOCRATES

And what of those who follow out of the course of nature, and are prodigies? for example, when a good and religious man has an irreligious son, he ought to bear the name not of his father, but of the class to which he belongs, just as in the case which was before supposed of a horse foaling a calf.

HERMOGENES

Quite true.

SOCRATES

Then the irreligious son of a religious father should be called irreligious?

HERMOGENES

Certainly.

SOCRATES

He should not be called Theophilus (beloved of God) or Mnesitheus (mindful of God), or any of these names: if names are correctly given, his should have an opposite meaning.

HERMOGENES

Certainly, Socrates.

SOCRATES

Again, Hermogenes, there is Orestes (the man of the mountains) who appears to be rightly called; whether chance gave the name, or perhaps some poet who meant to express the brutality and fierceness and mountain wildness of his hero's nature.

HERMOGENES

That is very likely, Socrates.

SOCRATES

And his father's name is also according to nature.

HERMOGENES

Clearly.

SOCRATES

Yes, for as his name, so also is his nature; Agamemnon (admirable for remaining) is one who is patient and persevering in the accomplishment of his resolves, and by his virtue crowns them; and his continuance at Troy with all the vast army is a proof of that admirable endurance in him which is signified by the name Agamemnon. I also think that Atreus is rightly called; for his murder of Chrysippus and his exceeding cruelty to Thyestes are damaging and destructive to his reputation--the name is a little altered and disguised so as not to be intelligible to every one, but to the etymologist there is no difficulty in seeing the meaning, for whether you think of him as ateires the stubborn, or as atrestos the fearless, or as ateros the destructive one, the name is perfectly correct in every point of view. And I think that Pelops is also named appropriately; for, as the name implies, he is rightly called Pelops who sees what is near only (o ta pelas oron).

HERMOGENES

How so?

SOCRATES

Because, according to the tradition, he had no forethought or foresight of all the evil which the murder of Myrtilus would entail upon his whole race in remote ages; he saw only what was at hand and immediate,--or in other words, pelas (near), in his eagerness to win Hippodamia by all means for his bride. Every one would agree that the name of Tantalus is rightly given and in accordance with nature, if the traditions about him are true.

HERMOGENES

And what are the traditions?

SOCRATES

Many terrible misfortunes are said to have happened to him in his life--last of all, came the utter ruin of his country; and after his death he had the stone suspended (talanteia) over his head in the world below--all this agrees wonderfully well with his name. You might imagine that some person who wanted to call him Talantatos (the most weighted down by misfortune), disguised the name by altering it into Tantalus; and into this form, by some accident of tradition, it has actually been transmuted. The name of Zeus, who is his alleged father, has also an excellent meaning, although hard to be understood, because really like a sentence, which is divided into two parts, for some call him Zena, and use the one half, and others who use the other half call him Dia; the two together signify the nature of the God, and the business of a name, as we were saying, is to express the nature. For there is none who is more the author of life to us and to all, than the lord and king of all. Wherefore we are right in calling him Zena and Dia, which are one name, although divided, meaning the God through whom all creatures always have life (di on zen aei pasi tois zosin uparchei). There is an irreverence, at first sight, in calling him son of Cronos (who is a proverb for stupidity), and we might rather expect Zeus to be the child of a mighty intellect. Which is the fact; for this is the meaning of his father's name: Kronos quasi Koros (Choreo, to sweep), not in the sense of a youth, but signifying to chatharon chai acheraton tou nou, the pure and garnished mind (sc. apo tou chorein). He, as we are informed by tradition, was begotten of Uranus, rightly so called (apo tou oran ta ano) from looking upwards; which, as philosophers tell us, is the way to have a pure mind, and the name Uranus is therefore correct. If I could remember the genealogy of Hesiod, I would have gone on and tried more conclusions of the same sort on the remoter ancestors of the Gods,--then I might have seen whether this wisdom, which has come to me all in an instant, I know not whence, will or will not hold good to the end.

HERMOGENES

You seem to me, Socrates, to be quite like a prophet newly inspired, and to be uttering oracles.

SOCRATES

Yes, Hermogenes, and I believe that I caught the inspiration from the great Euthyphro of the Prospaltian deme, who gave me a long lecture which commenced at dawn: he talked and I listened, and his wisdom and enchanting ravishment has not only filled my ears but taken possession of my soul, and to-day I shall let his superhuman power work and finish the investigation of names--that will be the way; but to-morrow, if you are so disposed, we will conjure him away, and make a purgation of him, if we can only find some priest or sophist who is skilled in purifications of this sort.

HERMOGENES

With all my heart; for am very curious to hear the rest of the enquiry about names.

SOCRATES
Then let us proceed; and where would you have us begin, now that we have got a sort of outline of the enquiry? Are there any names which witness of themselves that they are not given arbitrarily, but have a natural fitness? The names of heroes and of men in general are apt to be deceptive because they are often called after ancestors with whose names, as we were saying, they may have no business; or they are the expression of a wish like Eutychides (the son of good fortune), or Sosias (the Saviour), or Theophilus (the beloved of God), and others. But I think that we had better leave these, for there will be more chance of finding correctness in the names of immutable essences;--there ought to have been more care taken about them when they were named, and perhaps there may have been some more than human power at work occasionally in giving them names.

HERMOGENES
I think so, Socrates.

SOCRATES
Ought we not to begin with the consideration of the Gods, and show that they are rightly named Gods?

HERMOGENES
Yes, that will be well.

SOCRATES
My notion would be something of this sort:--I suspect that the sun, moon, earth, stars, and heaven, which are still the Gods of many barbarians, were the only Gods known to the aboriginal Hellenes. Seeing that they were always moving and running, from their running nature they were called Gods or runners (Theous, Theontas); and when men became acquainted with the other Gods, they proceeded to apply the same name to them all. Do you think that likely?

HERMOGENES
I think it very likely indeed.

SOCRATES
What shall follow the Gods?

HERMOGENES
Must not demons and heroes and men come next?

SOCRATES
Demons! And what do you consider to be the meaning of this word? Tell me if my view is right.

HERMOGENES
Let me hear.

SOCRATES
You know how Hesiod uses the word?

HERMOGENES

I do not.

SOCRATES
Do you not remember that he speaks of a golden race of men who came first?

HERMOGENES
Yes, I do.

SOCRATES
He says of them--

'But now that fate has closed over this race They are holy demons upon the earth, Beneficent, averters of ills, guardians of mortal men.' (Hesiod, Works and Days.)

HERMOGENES
What is the inference?

SOCRATES
What is the inference! Why, I suppose that he means by the golden men, not men literally made of gold, but good and noble; and I am convinced of this, because he further says that we are the iron race.

HERMOGENES
That is true.

SOCRATES
And do you not suppose that good men of our own day would by him be said to be of golden race?

HERMOGENES
Very likely.

SOCRATES
And are not the good wise?

HERMOGENES
Yes, they are wise.

SOCRATES
And therefore I have the most entire conviction that he called them demons, because they were daemones (knowing or wise), and in our older Attic dialect the word itself occurs. Now he and other poets say truly, that when a good man dies he has honour and a mighty portion among the dead, and becomes a demon; which is a name given to him signifying wisdom. And I say too, that every wise man who happens to be a good man is more than human (daimonion) both in life and death, and is rightly called a demon.

HERMOGENES
Then I rather think that I am of one mind with you; but what is the meaning of the word 'hero'? (Eros with an eta, in the old writing eros with an epsilon.)

SOCRATES

I think that there is no difficulty in explaining, for the name is not much altered, and signifies that they were born of love.

HERMOGENES

What do you mean?

SOCRATES

Do you not know that the heroes are demigods?

HERMOGENES

What then?

SOCRATES

All of them sprang either from the love of a God for a mortal woman, or of a mortal man for a Goddess; think of the word in the old Attic, and you will see better that the name heros is only a slight alteration of Eros, from whom the heroes sprang: either this is the meaning, or, if not this, then they must have been skilful as rhetoricians and dialecticians, and able to put the question (erotan), for eirein is equivalent to legein. And therefore, as I was saying, in the Attic dialect the heroes turn out to be rhetoricians and questioners. All this is easy enough; the noble breed of heroes are a tribe of sophists and rhetors. But can you tell me why men are called anthropoi?--that is more difficult.

HERMOGENES

No, I cannot; and I would not try even if I could, because I think that you are the more likely to succeed.

SOCRATES

That is to say, you trust to the inspiration of Euthyphro.

HERMOGENES

Of course.

SOCRATES

Your faith is not vain; for at this very moment a new and ingenious thought strikes me, and, if I am not careful, before to-morrow's dawn I shall be wiser than I ought to be. Now, attend to me; and first, remember that we often put in and pull out letters in words, and give names as we please and change the accents. Take, for example, the word Dii Philos; in order to convert this from a sentence into a noun, we omit one of the iotas and sound the middle syllable grave instead of acute; as, on the other hand, letters are sometimes inserted in words instead of being omitted, and the acute takes the place of the grave.

HERMOGENES

That is true.

SOCRATES

The name anthropos, which was once a sentence, and is now a noun, appears to be a case just of this sort, for one letter, which is the alpha, has been omitted, and the acute on the last syllable has been changed to a grave.

HERMOGENES

What do you mean?

SOCRATES

I mean to say that the word 'man' implies that other animals never examine, or consider, or look up at what they see, but that man not only sees (opope) but considers and looks up at that which he sees, and hence he alone of all animals is rightly anthropos, meaning anathron a opopen.

HERMOGENES

May I ask you to examine another word about which I am curious?

SOCRATES

Certainly.

HERMOGENES

I will take that which appears to me to follow next in order. You know the distinction of soul and body?

SOCRATES

Of course.

HERMOGENES

Let us endeavour to analyze them like the previous words.

SOCRATES

You want me first of all to examine the natural fitness of the word psuche (soul), and then of the word soma (body)?

HERMOGENES

Yes.

SOCRATES

If I am to say what occurs to me at the moment, I should imagine that those who first used the name psuche meant to express that the soul when in the body is the source of life, and gives the power of breath and revival (anapsuchon), and when this reviving power fails then the body perishes and dies, and this, if I am not mistaken, they called psyche. But please stay a moment; I fancy that I can discover something which will be more acceptable to the disciples of Euthyphro, for I am afraid that they will scorn this explanation. What do you say to another?

HERMOGENES

Let me hear.

SOCRATES

What is that which holds and carries and gives life and motion to the entire nature of the body? What else but the soul?

HERMOGENES

Just that.

SOCRATES

And do you not believe with Anaxagoras, that mind or soul is the ordering and containing principle of all things?

HERMOGENES

Yes; I do.

SOCRATES

Then you may well call that power phuseche which carries and holds nature (e phusin okei, kai ekei), and this may be refined away into psuche.

HERMOGENES

Certainly; and this derivation is, I think, more scientific than the other.

SOCRATES

It is so; but I cannot help laughing, if I am to suppose that this was the true meaning of the name.

HERMOGENES

But what shall we say of the next word?

SOCRATES

You mean soma (the body).

HERMOGENES

Yes.

SOCRATES

That may be variously interpreted; and yet more variously if a little permutation is allowed. For some say that the body is the grave (sema) of the soul which may be thought to be buried in our present life; or again the index of the soul, because the soul gives indications to (semainei) the body; probably the Orphic poets were the inventors of the name, and they were under the impression that the soul is suffering the punishment of sin, and that the body is an enclosure or prison in which the soul is incarcerated, kept safe (soma, sozetai), as the name soma implies, until the penalty is paid; according to this view, not even a letter of the word need be changed.

HERMOGENES

I think, Socrates, that we have said enough of this class of words. But have we any more explanations of the names of the Gods, like that which you were giving of Zeus? I should like to know whether any similar principle of correctness is to be applied to them.

SOCRATES

Yes, indeed, Hermogenes; and there is one excellent principle which, as men of sense, we must acknowledge,--that of the Gods we know nothing, either of their natures or of the names which they give themselves; but we are sure that the names by which they call themselves, whatever they may be, are true. And this is the best of all principles; and the next best is to say, as in prayers, that we will call them by any sort or kind of names or patronymics which they like, because we do not know of any other. That also, I think, is a very good custom, and one which I should much wish to observe. Let us, then, if you please, in the first place announce to them that we are not enquiring about them; we do not presume that we are able to do so; but we are enquiring about the meaning of men in giving them these names,--in this there can be small blame.

HERMOGENES

I think, Socrates, that you are quite right, and I would like to do as you say.

SOCRATES

Shall we begin, then, with Hestia, according to custom?

HERMOGENES

Yes, that will be very proper.

SOCRATES

What may we suppose him to have meant who gave the name Hestia?

HERMOGENES

That is another and certainly a most difficult question.

SOCRATES

My dear Hermogenes, the first imposers of names must surely have been considerable persons; they were philosophers, and had a good deal to say.

HERMOGENES

Well, and what of them?

SOCRATES

They are the men to whom I should attribute the imposition of names. Even in foreign names, if you analyze them, a meaning is still discernible. For example, that which we term ousia is by some called esia, and by others again osia. Now that the essence of things should be called estia, which is akin to the first of these (esia = estia), is rational enough. And there is reason in the Athenians calling that estia which participates in ousia. For in ancient times we too seem to have said esia for ousia, and this you may note to have been the idea of those who appointed that sacrifices should be first offered to estia, which was natural enough if they meant that estia was the essence of things. Those again who read osia seem to have inclined to the opinion of Heracleitus, that all things flow and nothing stands; with them the pushing principle (othoun) is the cause and ruling power of all things, and is therefore rightly called osia. Enough of this, which is all that we who know nothing can affirm. Next in order after Hestia we ought to consider Rhea and Cronos, although the name of Cronos has been already discussed. But I dare say that I am talking great nonsense.

HERMOGENES

Why, Socrates?

SOCRATES

My good friend, I have discovered a hive of wisdom.

HERMOGENES

Of what nature?

SOCRATES

Well, rather ridiculous, and yet plausible.

HERMOGENES

How plausible?

SOCRATES

I fancy to myself Heracleitus repeating wise traditions of antiquity as old as the days of Cronos and Rhea, and of which Homer also spoke.

HERMOGENES

How do you mean?

SOCRATES

Heracleitus is supposed to say that all things are in motion and nothing at rest; he compares them to the stream of a river, and says that you cannot go into the same water twice.

HERMOGENES

That is true.

SOCRATES

Well, then, how can we avoid inferring that he who gave the names of Cronos and Rhea to the ancestors of the Gods, agreed pretty much in the doctrine of Heracleitus? Is the giving of the names of streams to both of them purely accidental? Compare the line in which Homer, and, as I believe, Hesiod also, tells of

'Ocean, the origin of Gods, and mother Tethys (Il.--the line is not found in the extant works of Hesiod.).'

And again, Orpheus says, that

'The fair river of Ocean was the first to marry, and he espoused his sister Tethys, who was his mother's daughter.'

You see that this is a remarkable coincidence, and all in the direction of Heracleitus.

HERMOGENES

I think that there is something in what you say, Socrates; but I do not understand the meaning of the name Tethys.

SOCRATES

Well, that is almost self-explained, being only the name of a spring, a little disguised; for that which is strained and filtered (diattomenon, ethoumenon) may be likened to a spring, and the name Tethys is made up of these two words.

HERMOGENES

The idea is ingenious, Socrates.

SOCRATES

To be sure. But what comes next?--of Zeus we have spoken.

HERMOGENES

Yes.

SOCRATES

Then let us next take his two brothers, Poseidon and Pluto, whether the latter is called by that or by his other name.

HERMOGENES

By all means.

SOCRATES

Poseidon is Posidesmos, the chain of the feet; the original inventor of the name had been stopped by the watery element in his walks, and not allowed to go on, and therefore he called the ruler of this element Poseidon; the epsilon was probably inserted as an ornament. Yet, perhaps, not so; but the name may have been originally written with a double lamda and not with a sigma, meaning that the God knew many things (Polla eidos). And perhaps also he being the shaker of the earth, has been named from shaking (seiein), and then pi and delta have been added. Pluto gives wealth (Ploutos), and his name means the giver of wealth, which comes out of the earth beneath. People in general appear to imagine that the term Hades is connected with the invisible (aeides) and so they are led by their fears to call the God Pluto instead.

HERMOGENES

And what is the true derivation?

SOCRATES

In spite of the mistakes which are made about the power of this deity, and the foolish fears which people have of him, such as the fear of always being with him after death, and of the soul denuded of the body going to him (compare Rep.), my belief is that all is quite consistent, and that the office and name of the God really correspond.

HERMOGENES

Why, how is that?

SOCRATES

I will tell you my own opinion; but first, I should like to ask you which chain does any animal feel to be the stronger? and which confines him more to the same spot,--desire or necessity?

HERMOGENES

Desire, Socrates, is stronger far.

SOCRATES

And do you not think that many a one would escape from Hades, if he did not bind those who depart to him by the strongest of chains?

HERMOGENES

Assuredly they would.

SOCRATES

And if by the greatest of chains, then by some desire, as I should certainly infer, and not by necessity?

HERMOGENES

That is clear.

SOCRATES

And there are many desires?

HERMOGENES

Yes.

SOCRATES

And therefore by the greatest desire, if the chain is to be the greatest?

HERMOGENES

Yes.

SOCRATES

And is any desire stronger than the thought that you will be made better by associating with another?

HERMOGENES

Certainly not.

SOCRATES

And is not that the reason, Hermogenes, why no one, who has been to him, is willing to come back to us? Even the Sirens, like all the rest of the world, have been laid under his spells. Such a charm, as I imagine, is the God able to infuse into his words. And, according to this view, he is the perfect and accomplished Sophist, and the great benefactor of the inhabitants of the other world; and even to us who are upon earth he sends from below exceeding blessings. For he has much more than he wants down there; wherefore he is called Pluto (or the rich). Note also, that he will have nothing to do with men while they are in the body, but only when the soul is liberated from the desires and evils of the body. Now there is a great deal of philosophy and reflection in that; for in their liberated state he can bind them with the desire of virtue, but while they are flustered and maddened by the body, not even father Cronos himself would suffice to keep them with him in his own far-famed chains.

HERMOGENES

There is a deal of truth in what you say.

SOCRATES

Yes, Hermogenes, and the legislator called him Hades, not from the unseen (aeides)--far otherwise, but from his knowledge (eidenai) of all noble things.

HERMOGENES

Very good; and what do we say of Demeter, and Here, and Apollo, and Athene, and Hephaestus, and Ares, and the other deities?

SOCRATES

Demeter is e didousa meter, who gives food like a mother; Here is the lovely one (erate)--for Zeus, according to tradition, loved and married her; possibly also the name may have been given when the legislator was thinking of the heavens, and may be only a disguise of the air (aer), putting the end in the place of the beginning. You will recognize the truth of this if you repeat the letters of Here several times over. People dread the name of Pherephatta as they dread the name of Apollo,--and with as little reason; the fear, if I am not mistaken, only arises from their ignorance of the nature of names. But they go changing the name into Phersephone, and they are terrified at this; whereas the new name means only that the Goddess is wise (sophe); for seeing that all things in the world are in motion (pheromenon), that principle which embraces and touches and is able to follow them, is wisdom. And therefore the Goddess may be truly called Pherepaphe (Pherepapha), or some name like it, because she touches that which is in motion (tou pheromenon ephaptomene), herein showing her wisdom. And Hades, who is wise, consorts with her, because she is wise. They alter her name into Pherephatta now-a-days, because the present generation care for euphony more than truth. There is the other name, Apollo, which, as I was saying, is generally supposed to have some terrible signification. Have you remarked this fact?

HERMOGENES
To be sure I have, and what you say is true.

SOCRATES
But the name, in my opinion, is really most expressive of the power of the God.

HERMOGENES
How so?

SOCRATES
I will endeavour to explain, for I do not believe that any single name could have been better adapted to express the attributes of the God, embracing and in a manner signifying all four of them,--music, and prophecy, and medicine, and archery.

HERMOGENES
That must be a strange name, and I should like to hear the explanation.

SOCRATES
Say rather an harmonious name, as beseems the God of Harmony. In the first place, the purgations and purifications which doctors and diviners use, and their fumigations with drugs magical or medicinal, as well as their washings and lustral sprinklings, have all one and the same object, which is to make a man pure both in body and soul.

HERMOGENES
Very true.

SOCRATES
And is not Apollo the purifier, and the washer, and the absolver from all impurities?

HERMOGENES
Very true.

SOCRATES

Then in reference to his ablutions and absolutions, as being the physician who orders them, he may be rightly called Apolouon (purifier); or in respect of his powers of divination, and his truth and sincerity, which is the same as truth, he may be most fitly called Aplos, from aplous (sincere), as in the Thessalian dialect, for all the Thessalians call him Aplos; also he is aei Ballon (always shooting), because he is a master archer who never misses; or again, the name may refer to his musical attributes, and then, as in akolouthos, and akoitis, and in many other words the alpha is supposed to mean 'together,' so the meaning of the name Apollo will be 'moving together,' whether in the poles of heaven as they are called, or in the harmony of song, which is termed concord, because he moves all together by an harmonious power, as astronomers and musicians ingeniously declare. And he is the God who presides over harmony, and makes all things move together, both among Gods and among men. And as in the words akolouthos and akoitis the alpha is substituted for an omicron, so the name Apollon is equivalent to omopolon; only the second lambda is added in order to avoid the ill-omened sound of destruction (apolon). Now the suspicion of this destructive power still haunts the minds of some who do not consider the true value of the name, which, as I was saying just now, has reference to all the powers of the God, who is the single one, the everdarting, the purifier, the mover together (aplous, aei Ballon, apolouon, omopolon). The name of the Muses and of music would seem to be derived from their making philosophical enquiries (mosthai); and Leto is called by this name, because she is such a gentle Goddess, and so willing (ethelemon) to grant our requests; or her name may be Letho, as she is often called by strangers--they seem to imply by it her amiability, and her smooth and easy-going way of behaving. Artemis is named from her healthy (artemes), well-ordered nature, and because of her love of virginity, perhaps because she is a proficient in virtue (arete), and perhaps also as hating intercourse of the sexes (ton aroton misesasa). He who gave the Goddess her name may have had any or all of these reasons.

HERMOGENES

What is the meaning of Dionysus and Aphrodite?

SOCRATES

Son of Hipponicus, you ask a solemn question; there is a serious and also a facetious explanation of both these names; the serious explanation is not to be had from me, but there is no objection to your hearing the facetious one; for the Gods too love a joke. Dionusos is simply didous oinon (giver of wine), Didoinusos, as he might be called in fun,--and oinos is properly oionous, because wine makes those who drink, think (oiesthai) that they have a mind (noun) when they have none. The derivation of Aphrodite, born of the foam (aphros), may be fairly accepted on the authority of Hesiod.

HERMOGENES

Still there remains Athene, whom you, Socrates, as an Athenian, will surely not forget; there are also Hephaestus and Ares.

SOCRATES

I am not likely to forget them.

HERMOGENES

No, indeed.

SOCRATES

There is no difficulty in explaining the other appellation of Athene.

HERMOGENES

What other appellation?

SOCRATES

We call her Pallas.

HERMOGENES

To be sure.

SOCRATES

And we cannot be wrong in supposing that this is derived from armed dances. For the elevation of oneself or anything else above the earth, or by the use of the hands, we call shaking (pallein), or dancing.

HERMOGENES

That is quite true.

SOCRATES

Then that is the explanation of the name Pallas?

HERMOGENES

Yes; but what do you say of the other name?

SOCRATES

Athene?

HERMOGENES

Yes.

SOCRATES

That is a graver matter, and there, my friend, the modern interpreters of Homer may, I think, assist in explaining the view of the ancients. For most of these in their explanations of the poet, assert that he meant by Athene 'mind' (nous) and 'intelligence' (dianoia), and the maker of names appears to have had a singular notion about her; and indeed calls her by a still higher title, 'divine intelligence' (Thou noesis), as though he would say: This is she who has the mind of God (Theonoa);--using alpha as a dialectical variety for eta, and taking away iota and sigma (There seems to be some error in the MSS. The meaning is that the word theonoa = theounoa is a curtailed form of theou noesis, but the omitted letters do not agree.). Perhaps, however, the name Theonoe may mean 'she who knows divine things' (Theia noousa) better than others. Nor shall we be far wrong in supposing that the author of it wished to identify this Goddess with moral intelligence (en ethei noesin), and therefore gave her the name ethonoe; which, however, either he or his successors have altered into what they thought a nicer form, and called her Athene.

HERMOGENES

But what do you say of Hephaestus?

SOCRATES

Speak you of the princely lord of light (Phaeos istora)?

HERMOGENES
Surely.

SOCRATES
Ephaistos is Phaistos, and has added the eta by attraction; that is obvious to anybody.

HERMOGENES
That is very probable, until some more probable notion gets into your head.

SOCRATES
To prevent that, you had better ask what is the derivation of Ares.

HERMOGENES
What is Ares?

SOCRATES
Ares may be called, if you will, from his manhood (arren) and manliness, or if you please, from his hard and unchangeable nature, which is the meaning of arratos: the latter is a derivation in every way appropriate to the God of war.

HERMOGENES
Very true.

SOCRATES
And now, by the Gods, let us have no more of the Gods, for I am afraid of them; ask about anything but them, and thou shalt see how the steeds of Euthyphro can prance.

HERMOGENES
Only one more God! I should like to know about Hermes, of whom I am said not to be a true son. Let us make him out, and then I shall know whether there is any meaning in what Cratylus says.

SOCRATES
I should imagine that the name Hermes has to do with speech, and signifies that he is the interpreter (ermeneus), or messenger, or thief, or liar, or bargainer; all that sort of thing has a great deal to do with language; as I was telling you, the word eirein is expressive of the use of speech, and there is an often-recurring Homeric word emesato, which means 'he contrived'--out of these two words, eirein and mesasthai, the legislator formed the name of the God who invented language and speech; and we may imagine him dictating to us the use of this name: 'O my friends,' says he to us, 'seeing that he is the contriver of tales or speeches, you may rightly call him Eirhemes.' And this has been improved by us, as we think, into Hermes. Iris also appears to have been called from the verb 'to tell' (eirein), because she was a messenger.

HERMOGENES
Then I am very sure that Cratylus was quite right in saying that I was no true son of Hermes (Ermogenes), for I am not a good hand at speeches.

SOCRATES

There is also reason, my friend, in Pan being the double-formed son of Hermes.

HERMOGENES

How do you make that out?

SOCRATES

You are aware that speech signifies all things (pan), and is always turning them round and round, and has two forms, true and false?

HERMOGENES

Certainly.

SOCRATES

Is not the truth that is in him the smooth or sacred form which dwells above among the Gods, whereas falsehood dwells among men below, and is rough like the goat of tragedy; for tales and falsehoods have generally to do with the tragic or goatish life, and tragedy is the place of them?

HERMOGENES

Very true.

SOCRATES

Then surely Pan, who is the declarer of all things (pan) and the perpetual mover (aei polon) of all things, is rightly called aipolos (goat-herd), he being the two-formed son of Hermes, smooth in his upper part, and rough and goatlike in his lower regions. And, as the son of Hermes, he is speech or the brother of speech, and that brother should be like brother is no marvel. But, as I was saying, my dear Hermogenes, let us get away from the Gods.

HERMOGENES

From these sort of Gods, by all means, Socrates. But why should we not discuss another kind of Gods-- the sun, moon, stars, earth, aether, air, fire, water, the seasons, and the year?

SOCRATES

You impose a great many tasks upon me. Still, if you wish, I will not refuse.

HERMOGENES

You will oblige me.

SOCRATES

How would you have me begin? Shall I take first of all him whom you mentioned first--the sun?

HERMOGENES

Very good.

SOCRATES

The origin of the sun will probably be clearer in the Doric form, for the Dorians call him alios, and this name is given to him because when he rises he gathers (alizoi) men together or because he is always rolling in his course (aei eilein ion) about the earth; or from aiolein, of which the meaning is the same as poikillein (to variegate), because he variegates the productions of the earth.

HERMOGENES
But what is selene (the moon)?

SOCRATES
That name is rather unfortunate for Anaxagoras.

HERMOGENES
How so?

SOCRATES
The word seems to forestall his recent discovery, that the moon receives her light from the sun.

HERMOGENES
Why do you say so?

SOCRATES
The two words selas (brightness) and phos (light) have much the same meaning?

HERMOGENES
Yes.

SOCRATES
This light about the moon is always new (neon) and always old (enon), if the disciples of Anaxagoras say truly. For the sun in his revolution always adds new light, and there is the old light of the previous month.

HERMOGENES
Very true.

SOCRATES
The moon is not unfrequently called selanaia.

HERMOGENES
True.

SOCRATES
And as she has a light which is always old and always new (enon neon aei) she may very properly have the name selaenoneoaeia; and this when hammered into shape becomes selanaia.

HERMOGENES
A real dithyrambic sort of name that, Socrates. But what do you say of the month and the stars?

SOCRATES

Meis (month) is called from meiousthai (to lessen), because suffering diminution; the name of astra (stars) seems to be derived from astrape, which is an improvement on anastrope, signifying the upsetting of the eyes (anastrephein opa).

HERMOGENES
What do you say of pur (fire) and udor (water)?

SOCRATES
I am at a loss how to explain pur; either the muse of Euthyphro has deserted me, or there is some very great difficulty in the word. Please, however, to note the contrivance which I adopt whenever I am in a difficulty of this sort.

HERMOGENES
What is it?

SOCRATES
I will tell you; but I should like to know first whether you can tell me what is the meaning of the pur?

HERMOGENES
Indeed I cannot.

SOCRATES
Shall I tell you what I suspect to be the true explanation of this and several other words?--My belief is that they are of foreign origin. For the Hellenes, especially those who were under the dominion of the barbarians, often borrowed from them.

HERMOGENES
What is the inference?

SOCRATES
Why, you know that any one who seeks to demonstrate the fitness of these names according to the Hellenic language, and not according to the language from which the words are derived, is rather likely to be at fault.

HERMOGENES
Yes, certainly.

SOCRATES
Well then, consider whether this pur is not foreign; for the word is not easily brought into relation with the Hellenic tongue, and the Phrygians may be observed to have the same word slightly changed, just as they have udor (water) and kunes (dogs), and many other words.

HERMOGENES
That is true.

SOCRATES
Any violent interpretations of the words should be avoided; for something to say about them may easily be found. And thus I get rid of pur and udor. Aer (air), Hermogenes, may be explained as the element

which raises (airei) things from the earth, or as ever flowing (aei rei), or because the flux of the air is wind, and the poets call the winds 'air-blasts,' (aetai); he who uses the term may mean, so to speak, air-flux (aetorroun), in the sense of wind-flux (pneumatorroun); and because this moving wind may be expressed by either term he employs the word air (aer = aetes rheo). Aither (aether) I should interpret as aeitheer; this may be correctly said, because this element is always running in a flux about the air (aei thei peri tou aera reon). The meaning of the word ge (earth) comes out better when in the form of gaia, for the earth may be truly called 'mother' (gaia, genneteira), as in the language of Homer (Od.) gegaasi means gegennesthai.

HERMOGENES
Good.

SOCRATES
What shall we take next?

HERMOGENES
There are orai (the seasons), and the two names of the year, eniautos and etos.

SOCRATES
The orai should be spelt in the old Attic way, if you desire to know the probable truth about them; they are rightly called the orai because they divide (orizousin) the summers and winters and winds and the fruits of the earth. The words eniautos and etos appear to be the same,--'that which brings to light the plants and growths of the earth in their turn, and passes them in review within itself (en eauto exetazei)': this is broken up into two words, eniautos from en eauto, and etos from etazei, just as the original name of Zeus was divided into Zena and Dia; and the whole proposition means that his power of reviewing from within is one, but has two names, two words etos and eniautos being thus formed out of a single proposition.

HERMOGENES
Indeed, Socrates, you make surprising progress.

SOCRATES
I am run away with.

HERMOGENES
Very true.

SOCRATES
But am not yet at my utmost speed.

HERMOGENES
I should like very much to know, in the next place, how you would explain the virtues. What principle of correctness is there in those charming words--wisdom, understanding, justice, and the rest of them?

SOCRATES
That is a tremendous class of names which you are disinterring; still, as I have put on the lion's skin, I must not be faint of heart; and I suppose that I must consider the meaning of wisdom (phronesis) and

understanding (sunesis), and judgment (gnome), and knowledge (episteme), and all those other charming words, as you call them?

HERMOGENES
Surely, we must not leave off until we find out their meaning.

SOCRATES
By the dog of Egypt I have a not bad notion which came into my head only this moment: I believe that the primeval givers of names were undoubtedly like too many of our modern philosophers, who, in their search after the nature of things, are always getting dizzy from constantly going round and round, and then they imagine that the world is going round and round and moving in all directions; and this appearance, which arises out of their own internal condition, they suppose to be a reality of nature; they think that there is nothing stable or permanent, but only flux and motion, and that the world is always full of every sort of motion and change. The consideration of the names which I mentioned has led me into making this reflection.

HERMOGENES
How is that, Socrates?

SOCRATES
Perhaps you did not observe that in the names which have been just cited, the motion or flux or generation of things is most surely indicated.

HERMOGENES
No, indeed, I never thought of it.

SOCRATES
Take the first of those which you mentioned; clearly that is a name indicative of motion.

HERMOGENES
What was the name?

SOCRATES
Phronesis (wisdom), which may signify phoras kai rhou noesis (perception of motion and flux), or perhaps phoras onesis (the blessing of motion), but is at any rate connected with pheresthai (motion); gnome (judgment), again, certainly implies the ponderation or consideration (nomesis) of generation, for to ponder is the same as to consider; or, if you would rather, here is noesis, the very word just now mentioned, which is neou esis (the desire of the new); the word neos implies that the world is always in process of creation. The giver of the name wanted to express this longing of the soul, for the original name was neoesis, and not noesis; but eta took the place of a double epsilon. The word sophrosune is the salvation (soteria) of that wisdom (phronesis) which we were just now considering. Epioteme (knowledge) is akin to this, and indicates that the soul which is good for anything follows (epetai) the motion of things, neither anticipating them nor falling behind them; wherefore the word should rather be read as epistemene, inserting epsilon nu. Sunesis (understanding) may be regarded in like manner as a kind of conclusion; the word is derived from sunienai (to go along with), and, like epistasthai (to know), implies the progression of the soul in company with the nature of things. Sophia (wisdom) is very dark, and appears not to be of native growth; the meaning is, touching the motion or stream of things. You must remember that the poets, when they speak of the commencement of any rapid motion, often

use the word esuthe (he rushed); and there was a famous Lacedaemonian who was named Sous (Rush), for by this word the Lacedaemonians signify rapid motion, and the touching (epaphe) of motion is expressed by sophia, for all things are supposed to be in motion. Good (agathon) is the name which is given to the admirable (agasto) in nature; for, although all things move, still there are degrees of motion; some are swifter, some slower; but there are some things which are admirable for their swiftness, and this admirable part of nature is called agathon. Dikaiosune (justice) is clearly dikaiou sunesis (understanding of the just); but the actual word dikaion is more difficult: men are only agreed to a certain extent about justice, and then they begin to disagree. For those who suppose all things to be in motion conceive the greater part of nature to be a mere receptacle; and they say that there is a penetrating power which passes through all this, and is the instrument of creation in all, and is the subtlest and swiftest element; for if it were not the subtlest, and a power which none can keep out, and also the swiftest, passing by other things as if they were standing still, it could not penetrate through the moving universe. And this element, which superintends all things and pierces (diaion) all, is rightly called dikaion; the letter k is only added for the sake of euphony. Thus far, as I was saying, there is a general agreement about the nature of justice; but I, Hermogenes, being an enthusiastic disciple, have been told in a mystery that the justice of which I am speaking is also the cause of the world: now a cause is that because of which anything is created; and some one comes and whispers in my ear that justice is rightly so called because partaking of the nature of the cause, and I begin, after hearing what he has said, to interrogate him gently: 'Well, my excellent friend,' say I, 'but if all this be true, I still want to know what is justice.' Thereupon they think that I ask tiresome questions, and am leaping over the barriers, and have been already sufficiently answered, and they try to satisfy me with one derivation after another, and at length they quarrel. For one of them says that justice is the sun, and that he only is the piercing (diaionta) and burning (kaonta) element which is the guardian of nature. And when I joyfully repeat this beautiful notion, I am answered by the satirical remark, 'What, is there no justice in the world when the sun is down?' And when I earnestly beg my questioner to tell me his own honest opinion, he says, 'Fire in the abstract'; but this is not very intelligible. Another says, 'No, not fire in the abstract, but the abstraction of heat in the fire.' Another man professes to laugh at all this, and says, as Anaxagoras says, that justice is mind, for mind, as they say, has absolute power, and mixes with nothing, and orders all things, and passes through all things. At last, my friend, I find myself in far greater perplexity about the nature of justice than I was before I began to learn. But still I am of opinion that the name, which has led me into this digression, was given to justice for the reasons which I have mentioned.

HERMOGENES
I think, Socrates, that you are not improvising now; you must have heard this from some one else.

SOCRATES
And not the rest?

HERMOGENES
Hardly.

SOCRATES
Well, then, let me go on in the hope of making you believe in the originality of the rest. What remains after justice? I do not think that we have as yet discussed courage (andreia),--injustice (adikia), which is obviously nothing more than a hindrance to the penetrating principle (diaiontos), need not be considered. Well, then, the name of andreia seems to imply a battle;--this battle is in the world of existence, and according to the doctrine of flux is only the counterflux (enantia rhon): if you extract the delta from andreia, the name at once signifies the thing, and you may clearly understand that andreia is

not the stream opposed to every stream, but only to that which is contrary to justice, for otherwise courage would not have been praised. The words arren (male) and aner (man) also contain a similar allusion to the same principle of the upward flux (te ano rhon). Gune (woman) I suspect to be the same word as goun (birth): thelu (female) appears to be partly derived from thele (the teat), because the teat is like rain, and makes things flourish (tethelenai).

HERMOGENES
That is surely probable.

SOCRATES
Yes; and the very word thallein (to flourish) seems to figure the growth of youth, which is swift and sudden ever. And this is expressed by the legislator in the name, which is a compound of thein (running), and allesthai (leaping). Pray observe how I gallop away when I get on smooth ground. There are a good many names generally thought to be of importance, which have still to be explained.

HERMOGENES
True.

SOCRATES
There is the meaning of the word techne (art), for example.

HERMOGENES
Very true.

SOCRATES
That may be identified with echonoe, and expresses the possession of mind: you have only to take away the tau and insert two omichrons, one between the chi and nu, and another between the nu and eta.

HERMOGENES
That is a very shabby etymology.

SOCRATES
Yes, my dear friend; but then you know that the original names have been long ago buried and disguised by people sticking on and stripping off letters for the sake of euphony, and twisting and bedizening them in all sorts of ways: and time too may have had a share in the change. Take, for example, the word katoptron; why is the letter rho inserted? This must surely be the addition of some one who cares nothing about the truth, but thinks only of putting the mouth into shape. And the additions are often such that at last no human being can possibly make out the original meaning of the word. Another example is the word sphigx, sphiggos, which ought properly to be phigx, phiggos, and there are other examples.

HERMOGENES
That is quite true, Socrates.

SOCRATES
And yet, if you are permitted to put in and pull out any letters which you please, names will be too easily made, and any name may be adapted to any object.

HERMOGENES

True.

SOCRATES

Yes, that is true. And therefore a wise dictator, like yourself, should observe the laws of moderation and probability.

HERMOGENES

Such is my desire.

SOCRATES

And mine, too, Hermogenes. But do not be too much of a precisian, or 'you will unnerve me of my strength (Iliad.).' When you have allowed me to add mechane (contrivance) to techne (art) I shall be at the top of my bent, for I conceive mechane to be a sign of great accomplishment--anein; for mekos has the meaning of greatness, and these two, mekos and anein, make up the word mechane. But, as I was saying, being now at the top of my bent, I should like to consider the meaning of the two words arete (virtue) and kakia (vice); arete I do not as yet understand, but kakia is transparent, and agrees with the principles which preceded, for all things being in a flux (ionton), kakia is kakos ion (going badly); and this evil motion when existing in the soul has the general name of kakia, or vice, specially appropriated to it. The meaning of kakos ienai may be further illustrated by the use of deilia (cowardice), which ought to have come after andreia, but was forgotten, and, as I fear, is not the only word which has been passed over. Deilia signifies that the soul is bound with a strong chain (desmos), for lian means strength, and therefore deilia expresses the greatest and strongest bond of the soul; and aporia (difficulty) is an evil of the same nature (from a (alpha) not, and poreuesthai to go), like anything else which is an impediment to motion and movement. Then the word kakia appears to mean kakos ienai, or going badly, or limping and halting; of which the consequence is, that the soul becomes filled with vice. And if kakia is the name of this sort of thing, arete will be the opposite of it, signifying in the first place ease of motion, then that the stream of the good soul is unimpeded, and has therefore the attribute of ever flowing without let or hindrance, and is therefore called arete, or, more correctly, aeireite (ever-flowing), and may perhaps have had another form, airete (eligible), indicating that nothing is more eligible than virtue, and this has been hammered into arete. I daresay that you will deem this to be another invention of mine, but I think that if the previous word kakia was right, then arete is also right.

HERMOGENES

But what is the meaning of kakon, which has played so great a part in your previous discourse?

SOCRATES

That is a very singular word about which I can hardly form an opinion, and therefore I must have recourse to my ingenious device.

HERMOGENES

What device?

SOCRATES

The device of a foreign origin, which I shall give to this word also.

HERMOGENES

Very likely you are right; but suppose that we leave these words and endeavour to see the rationale of kalon and aischron.

SOCRATES
The meaning of aischron is evident, being only aei ischon roes (always preventing from flowing), and this is in accordance with our former derivations. For the name-giver was a great enemy to stagnation of all sorts, and hence he gave the name aeischoroun to that which hindered the flux (aei ischon roun), and that is now beaten together into aischron.

HERMOGENES
But what do you say of kalon?

SOCRATES
That is more obscure; yet the form is only due to the quantity, and has been changed by altering omicron upsilon into omicron.

HERMOGENES
What do you mean?

SOCRATES
This name appears to denote mind.

HERMOGENES
How so?

SOCRATES
Let me ask you what is the cause why anything has a name; is not the principle which imposes the name the cause?

HERMOGENES
Certainly.

SOCRATES
And must not this be the mind of Gods, or of men, or of both?

HERMOGENES
Yes.

SOCRATES
Is not mind that which called (kalesan) things by their names, and is not mind the beautiful (kalon)?

HERMOGENES
That is evident.

SOCRATES
And are not the works of intelligence and mind worthy of praise, and are not other works worthy of blame?

HERMOGENES

Certainly.

SOCRATES

Physic does the work of a physician, and carpentering does the works of a carpenter?

HERMOGENES

Exactly.

SOCRATES

And the principle of beauty does the works of beauty?

HERMOGENES

Of course.

SOCRATES

And that principle we affirm to be mind?

HERMOGENES

Very true.

SOCRATES

Then mind is rightly called beauty because she does the works which we recognize and speak of as the beautiful?

HERMOGENES

That is evident.

SOCRATES

What more names remain to us?

HERMOGENES

There are the words which are connected with agathon and kalon, such as sumpheron and lusiteloun, ophelimon, kerdaleon, and their opposites.

SOCRATES

The meaning of sumpheron (expedient) I think that you may discover for yourself by the light of the previous examples,--for it is a sister word to episteme, meaning just the motion (pora) of the soul accompanying the world, and things which are done upon this principle are called sumphora or sumpheronta, because they are carried round with the world.

HERMOGENES

That is probable.

SOCRATES

Again, cherdaleon (gainful) is called from cherdos (gain), but you must alter the delta into nu if you want to get at the meaning; for this word also signifies good, but in another way; he who gave the name intended to express the power of admixture (kerannumenon) and universal penetration in the good; in forming the word, however, he inserted a delta instead of a nu, and so made kerdos.

HERMOGENES
Well, but what is lusiteloun (profitable)?

SOCRATES
I suppose, Hermogenes, that people do not mean by the profitable the gainful or that which pays (luei) the retailer, but they use the word in the sense of swift. You regard the profitable (lusiteloun), as that which being the swiftest thing in existence, allows of no stay in things and no pause or end of motion, but always, if there begins to be any end, lets things go again (luei), and makes motion immortal and unceasing: and in this point of view, as appears to me, the good is happily denominated lusiteloun-- being that which looses (luon) the end (telos) of motion. Ophelimon (the advantageous) is derived from ophellein, meaning that which creates and increases; this latter is a common Homeric word, and has a foreign character.

HERMOGENES
And what do you say of their opposites?

SOCRATES
Of such as are mere negatives I hardly think that I need speak.

HERMOGENES
Which are they?

SOCRATES
The words axumphoron (inexpedient), anopheles (unprofitable), alusiteles (unadvantageous), akerdes (ungainful).

HERMOGENES
True.

SOCRATES
I would rather take the words blaberon (harmful), zemiodes (hurtful).

HERMOGENES
Good.

SOCRATES
The word blaberon is that which is said to hinder or harm (blaptein) the stream (roun); blapton is boulomenon aptein (seeking to hold or bind); for aptein is the same as dein, and dein is always a term of censure; boulomenon aptein roun (wanting to bind the stream) would properly be boulapteroun, and this, as I imagine, is improved into blaberon.

HERMOGENES
You bring out curious results, Socrates, in the use of names; and when I hear the word boulapteroun I cannot help imagining that you are making your mouth into a flute, and puffing away at some prelude to Athene.

SOCRATES

That is the fault of the makers of the name, Hermogenes; not mine.

HERMOGENES

Very true; but what is the derivation of zemiodes?

SOCRATES

What is the meaning of zemiodes?--let me remark, Hermogenes, how right I was in saying that great changes are made in the meaning of words by putting in and pulling out letters; even a very slight permutation will sometimes give an entirely opposite sense; I may instance the word deon, which occurs to me at the moment, and reminds me of what I was going to say to you, that the fine fashionable language of modern times has twisted and disguised and entirely altered the original meaning both of deon, and also of zemiodes, which in the old language is clearly indicated.

HERMOGENES

What do you mean?

SOCRATES

I will try to explain. You are aware that our forefathers loved the sounds iota and delta, especially the women, who are most conservative of the ancient language, but now they change iota into eta or epsilon, and delta into zeta; this is supposed to increase the grandeur of the sound.

HERMOGENES

How do you mean?

SOCRATES

For example, in very ancient times they called the day either imera or emera (short e), which is called by us emera (long e).

HERMOGENES

That is true.

SOCRATES

Do you observe that only the ancient form shows the intention of the giver of the name? of which the reason is, that men long for (imeirousi) and love the light which comes after the darkness, and is therefore called imera, from imeros, desire.

HERMOGENES

Clearly.

SOCRATES

But now the name is so travestied that you cannot tell the meaning, although there are some who imagine the day to be called emera because it makes things gentle (emera different accents).

HERMOGENES

Such is my view.

SOCRATES

And do you know that the ancients said duogon and not zugon?

HERMOGENES

They did so.

SOCRATES

And zugon (yoke) has no meaning,--it ought to be duogon, which word expresses the binding of two together (duein agoge) for the purpose of drawing;--this has been changed into zugon, and there are many other examples of similar changes.

HERMOGENES

There are.

SOCRATES

Proceeding in the same train of thought I may remark that the word deon (obligation) has a meaning which is the opposite of all the other appellations of good; for deon is here a species of good, and is, nevertheless, the chain (desmos) or hinderer of motion, and therefore own brother of blaberon.

HERMOGENES

Yes, Socrates; that is quite plain.

SOCRATES

Not if you restore the ancient form, which is more likely to be the correct one, and read dion instead of deon; if you convert the epsilon into an iota after the old fashion, this word will then agree with other words meaning good; for dion, not deon, signifies the good, and is a term of praise; and the author of names has not contradicted himself, but in all these various appellations, deon (obligatory), ophelimon (advantageous), lusiteloun (profitable), kerdaleon (gainful), agathon (good), sumpheron (expedient), euporon (plenteous), the same conception is implied of the ordering or all-pervading principle which is praised, and the restraining and binding principle which is censured. And this is further illustrated by the word zemiodes (hurtful), which if the zeta is only changed into delta as in the ancient language, becomes demiodes; and this name, as you will perceive, is given to that which binds motion (dounti ion).

HERMOGENES

What do you say of edone (pleasure), lupe (pain), epithumia (desire), and the like, Socrates?

SOCRATES

I do not think, Hermogenes, that there is any great difficulty about them--edone is e (eta) onesis, the action which tends to advantage; and the original form may be supposed to have been eone, but this has been altered by the insertion of the delta. Lupe appears to be derived from the relaxation (luein) which the body feels when in sorrow; ania (trouble) is the hindrance of motion (alpha and ienai); algedon (distress), if I am not mistaken, is a foreign word, which is derived from aleinos (grievous); odune (grief) is called from the putting on (endusis) sorrow; in achthedon (vexation) 'the word too labours,' as any one may see; chara (joy) is the very expression of the fluency and diffusion of the soul (cheo); terpsis (delight) is so called from the pleasure creeping (erpon) through the soul, which may be likened to a breath (pnoe) and is properly erpnoun, but has been altered by time into terpnon; eupherosune (cheerfulness) and epithumia explain themselves; the former, which ought to be eupherosune and has been changed euphrosune, is named, as every one may see, from the soul moving (pheresthai) in harmony with nature; epithumia is really e epi ton thumon iousa dunamis, the power which enters into the soul; thumos (passion) is called from the rushing (thuseos) and boiling of the soul; imeros (desire) denotes the stream (rous) which most draws the soul dia ten esin tes roes--because flowing with desire (iemenos), and expresses a longing after things and violent attraction of the soul to them, and is termed imeros from possessing this power; pothos (longing) is expressive of the desire of that which is not present but absent, and in another place (pou); this is the reason why the name pothos is applied to things absent, as imeros is to things present; eros (love) is so called because flowing in (esron) from without; the stream is not inherent, but is an influence introduced through the eyes, and from flowing in was called esros (influx) in the old time when they used omicron for omega, and is called eros, now that omega is substituted for omicron. But why do you not give me another word?

HERMOGENES
What do you think of doxa (opinion), and that class of words?

SOCRATES
Doxa is either derived from dioxis (pursuit), and expresses the march of the soul in the pursuit of knowledge, or from the shooting of a bow (toxon); the latter is more likely, and is confirmed by oiesis (thinking), which is only oisis (moving), and implies the movement of the soul to the essential nature of each thing--just as boule (counsel) has to do with shooting (bole); and boulesthai (to wish) combines the notion of aiming and deliberating--all these words seem to follow doxa, and all involve the idea of shooting, just as aboulia, absence of counsel, on the other hand, is a mishap, or missing, or mistaking of the mark, or aim, or proposal, or object.

HERMOGENES
You are quickening your pace now, Socrates.

SOCRATES
Why yes, the end I now dedicate to God, not, however, until I have explained anagke (necessity), which ought to come next, and ekousion (the voluntary). Ekousion is certainly the yielding (eikon) and unresisting--the notion implied is yielding and not opposing, yielding, as I was just now saying, to that motion which is in accordance with our will; but the necessary and resistant being contrary to our will, implies error and ignorance; the idea is taken from walking through a ravine which is impassable, and rugged, and overgrown, and impedes motion--and this is the derivation of the word anagkaion (necessary) an agke ion, going through a ravine. But while my strength lasts let us persevere, and I hope that you will persevere with your questions.

HERMOGENES
Well, then, let me ask about the greatest and noblest, such as aletheia (truth) and pseudos (falsehood) and on (being), not forgetting to enquire why the word onoma (name), which is the theme of our discussion, has this name of onoma.

SOCRATES
You know the word maiesthai (to seek)?

HERMOGENES
Yes;--meaning the same as zetein (to enquire).

SOCRATES

The word onoma seems to be a compressed sentence, signifying on ou zetema (being for which there is a search); as is still more obvious in onomaston (notable), which states in so many words that real existence is that for which there is a seeking (on ou masma); aletheia is also an agglomeration of theia ale (divine wandering), implying the divine motion of existence; pseudos (falsehood) is the opposite of motion; here is another ill name given by the legislator to stagnation and forced inaction, which he compares to sleep (eudein); but the original meaning of the word is disguised by the addition of psi; on and ousia are ion with an iota broken off; this agrees with the true principle, for being (on) is also moving (ion), and the same may be said of not being, which is likewise called not going (oukion or ouki on = ouk ion).

HERMOGENES
You have hammered away at them manfully; but suppose that some one were to say to you, what is the word ion, and what are reon and doun?--show me their fitness.

SOCRATES
You mean to say, how should I answer him?

HERMOGENES
Yes.

SOCRATES
One way of giving the appearance of an answer has been already suggested.

HERMOGENES
What way?

SOCRATES
To say that names which we do not understand are of foreign origin; and this is very likely the right answer, and something of this kind may be true of them; but also the original forms of words may have been lost in the lapse of ages; names have been so twisted in all manner of ways, that I should not be surprised if the old language when compared with that now in use would appear to us to be a barbarous tongue.

HERMOGENES
Very likely.

SOCRATES
Yes, very likely. But still the enquiry demands our earnest attention and we must not flinch. For we should remember, that if a person go on analysing names into words, and enquiring also into the elements out of which the words are formed, and keeps on always repeating this process, he who has to answer him must at last give up the enquiry in despair.

HERMOGENES
Very true.

SOCRATES
And at what point ought he to lose heart and give up the enquiry? Must he not stop when he comes to the names which are the elements of all other names and sentences; for these cannot be supposed to

be made up of other names? The word agathon (good), for example, is, as we were saying, a compound of agastos (admirable) and thoos (swift). And probably thoos is made up of other elements, and these again of others. But if we take a word which is incapable of further resolution, then we shall be right in saying that we have at last reached a primary element, which need not be resolved any further.

HERMOGENES
I believe you to be in the right.

SOCRATES
And suppose the names about which you are now asking should turn out to be primary elements, must not their truth or law be examined according to some new method?

HERMOGENES
Very likely.

SOCRATES
Quite so, Hermogenes; all that has preceded would lead to this conclusion. And if, as I think, the conclusion is true, then I shall again say to you, come and help me, that I may not fall into some absurdity in stating the principle of primary names.

HERMOGENES
Let me hear, and I will do my best to assist you.

SOCRATES
I think that you will acknowledge with me, that one principle is applicable to all names, primary as well as secondary--when they are regarded simply as names, there is no difference in them.

HERMOGENES
Certainly not.

SOCRATES
All the names that we have been explaining were intended to indicate the nature of things.

HERMOGENES
Of course.

SOCRATES
And that this is true of the primary quite as much as of the secondary names, is implied in their being names.

HERMOGENES
Surely.

SOCRATES
But the secondary, as I conceive, derive their significance from the primary.

HERMOGENES
That is evident.

SOCRATES

Very good; but then how do the primary names which precede analysis show the natures of things, as far as they can be shown; which they must do, if they are to be real names? And here I will ask you a question: Suppose that we had no voice or tongue, and wanted to communicate with one another, should we not, like the deaf and dumb, make signs with the hands and head and the rest of the body?

HERMOGENES

There would be no choice, Socrates.

SOCRATES

We should imitate the nature of the thing; the elevation of our hands to heaven would mean lightness and upwardness; heaviness and downwardness would be expressed by letting them drop to the ground; if we were describing the running of a horse, or any other animal, we should make our bodies and their gestures as like as we could to them.

HERMOGENES

I do not see that we could do anything else.

SOCRATES

We could not; for by bodily imitation only can the body ever express anything.

HERMOGENES

Very true.

SOCRATES

And when we want to express ourselves, either with the voice, or tongue, or mouth, the expression is simply their imitation of that which we want to express.

HERMOGENES

It must be so, I think.

SOCRATES

Then a name is a vocal imitation of that which the vocal imitator names or imitates?

HERMOGENES

I think so.

SOCRATES

Nay, my friend, I am disposed to think that we have not reached the truth as yet.

HERMOGENES

Why not?

SOCRATES

Because if we have we shall be obliged to admit that the people who imitate sheep, or cocks, or other animals, name that which they imitate.

HERMOGENES

Quite true.

SOCRATES

Then could I have been right in what I was saying?

HERMOGENES

In my opinion, no. But I wish that you would tell me, Socrates, what sort of an imitation is a name?

SOCRATES

In the first place, I should reply, not a musical imitation, although that is also vocal; nor, again, an imitation of what music imitates; these, in my judgment, would not be naming. Let me put the matter as follows: All objects have sound and figure, and many have colour?

HERMOGENES

Certainly.

SOCRATES

But the art of naming appears not to be concerned with imitations of this kind; the arts which have to do with them are music and drawing?

HERMOGENES

True.

SOCRATES

Again, is there not an essence of each thing, just as there is a colour, or sound? And is there not an essence of colour and sound as well as of anything else which may be said to have an essence?

HERMOGENES

I should think so.

SOCRATES

Well, and if any one could express the essence of each thing in letters and syllables, would he not express the nature of each thing?

HERMOGENES

Quite so.

SOCRATES

The musician and the painter were the two names which you gave to the two other imitators. What will this imitator be called?

HERMOGENES

I imagine, Socrates, that he must be the namer, or name-giver, of whom we are in search.

SOCRATES

If this is true, then I think that we are in a condition to consider the names ron (stream), ienai (to go), schesis (retention), about which you were asking; and we may see whether the namer has grasped the nature of them in letters and syllables in such a manner as to imitate the essence or not.

HERMOGENES
Very good.

SOCRATES
But are these the only primary names, or are there others?

HERMOGENES
There must be others.

SOCRATES
So I should expect. But how shall we further analyse them, and where does the imitator begin? Imitation of the essence is made by syllables and letters; ought we not, therefore, first to separate the letters, just as those who are beginning rhythm first distinguish the powers of elementary, and then of compound sounds, and when they have done so, but not before, they proceed to the consideration of rhythms?

HERMOGENES
Yes.

SOCRATES
Must we not begin in the same way with letters; first separating the vowels, and then the consonants and mutes (letters which are neither vowels nor semivowels), into classes, according to the received distinctions of the learned; also the semivowels, which are neither vowels, nor yet mutes; and distinguishing into classes the vowels themselves? And when we have perfected the classification of things, we shall give them names, and see whether, as in the case of letters, there are any classes to which they may be all referred (cf. Phaedrus); and hence we shall see their natures, and see, too, whether they have in them classes as there are in the letters; and when we have well considered all this, we shall know how to apply them to what they resemble--whether one letter is used to denote one thing, or whether there is to be an admixture of several of them; just, as in painting, the painter who wants to depict anything sometimes uses purple only, or any other colour, and sometimes mixes up several colours, as his method is when he has to paint flesh colour or anything of that kind--he uses his colours as his figures appear to require them; and so, too, we shall apply letters to the expression of objects, either single letters when required, or several letters; and so we shall form syllables, as they are called, and from syllables make nouns and verbs; and thus, at last, from the combinations of nouns and verbs arrive at language, large and fair and whole; and as the painter made a figure, even so shall we make speech by the art of the namer or the rhetorician, or by some other art. Not that I am literally speaking of ourselves, but I was carried away--meaning to say that this was the way in which (not we but) the ancients formed language, and what they put together we must take to pieces in like manner, if we are to attain a scientific view of the whole subject, and we must see whether the primary, and also whether the secondary elements are rightly given or not, for if they are not, the composition of them, my dear Hermogenes, will be a sorry piece of work, and in the wrong direction.

HERMOGENES
That, Socrates, I can quite believe.

SOCRATES

Well, but do you suppose that you will be able to analyse them in this way? for I am certain that I should not.

HERMOGENES

Much less am I likely to be able.

SOCRATES

Shall we leave them, then? or shall we seek to discover, if we can, something about them, according to the measure of our ability, saying by way of preface, as I said before of the Gods, that of the truth about them we know nothing, and do but entertain human notions of them. And in this present enquiry, let us say to ourselves, before we proceed, that the higher method is the one which we or others who would analyse language to any good purpose must follow; but under the circumstances, as men say, we must do as well as we can. What do you think?

HERMOGENES

I very much approve.

SOCRATES

That objects should be imitated in letters and syllables, and so find expression, may appear ridiculous, Hermogenes, but it cannot be avoided--there is no better principle to which we can look for the truth of first names. Deprived of this, we must have recourse to divine help, like the tragic poets, who in any perplexity have their gods waiting in the air; and must get out of our difficulty in like fashion, by saying that 'the Gods gave the first names, and therefore they are right.' This will be the best contrivance, or perhaps that other notion may be even better still, of deriving them from some barbarous people, for the barbarians are older than we are; or we may say that antiquity has cast a veil over them, which is the same sort of excuse as the last; for all these are not reasons but only ingenious excuses for having no reasons concerning the truth of words. And yet any sort of ignorance of first or primitive names involves an ignorance of secondary words; for they can only be explained by the primary. Clearly then the professor of languages should be able to give a very lucid explanation of first names, or let him be assured he will only talk nonsense about the rest. Do you not suppose this to be true?

HERMOGENES

Certainly, Socrates.

SOCRATES

My first notions of original names are truly wild and ridiculous, though I have no objection to impart them to you if you desire, and I hope that you will communicate to me in return anything better which you may have.

HERMOGENES

Fear not; I will do my best.

SOCRATES

In the first place, the letter rho appears to me to be the general instrument expressing all motion (kinesis). But I have not yet explained the meaning of this latter word, which is just iesis (going); for the letter eta was not in use among the ancients, who only employed epsilon; and the root is kiein, which is a foreign form, the same as ienai. And the old word kinesis will be correctly given as iesis in corresponding modern letters. Assuming this foreign root kiein, and allowing for the change of the eta and the insertion of the nu, we have kinesis, which should have been kieinsis or eisis; and stasis is the negative of ienai (or eisis), and has been improved into stasis. Now the letter rho, as I was saying, appeared to the imposer of names an excellent instrument for the expression of motion; and he frequently uses the letter for this purpose: for example, in the actual words rein and roe he represents motion by rho; also in the words tromos (trembling), trachus (rugged); and again, in words such as krouein (strike), thrauein (crush), ereikein (bruise), thruptein (break), kermatixein (crumble), rumbein (whirl): of all these sorts of movements he generally finds an expression in the letter R, because, as I imagine, he had observed that the tongue was most agitated and least at rest in the pronunciation of this letter, which he therefore used in order to express motion, just as by the letter iota he expresses the subtle elements which pass through all things. This is why he uses the letter iota as imitative of motion, ienai, iesthai. And there is another class of letters, phi, psi, sigma, and xi, of which the pronunciation is accompanied by great expenditure of breath; these are used in the imitation of such notions as psuchron (shivering), xeon (seething), seiesthai, (to be shaken), seismos (shock), and are always introduced by the giver of names when he wants to imitate what is phusodes (windy). He seems to have thought that the closing and pressure of the tongue in the utterance of delta and tau was expressive of binding and rest in a place: he further observed the liquid movement of lambda, in the pronunciation of which the tongue slips, and in this he found the expression of smoothness, as in leios (level), and in the word oliothanein (to slip) itself, liparon (sleek), in the word kollodes (gluey), and the like: the heavier sound of gamma detained the slipping tongue, and the union of the two gave the notion of a glutinous clammy nature, as in glischros, glukus, gloiodes. The nu he observed to be sounded from within, and therefore to have a notion of inwardness; hence he introduced the sound in endos and entos: alpha he assigned to the expression of size, and nu of length, because they are great letters: omicron was the sign of roundness, and therefore there is plenty of omicron mixed up in the word goggulon (round). Thus did the legislator, reducing all things into letters and syllables, and impressing on them names and signs, and out of them by imitation compounding other signs. That is my view, Hermogenes, of the truth of names; but I should like to hear what Cratylus has more to say.

HERMOGENES
But, Socrates, as I was telling you before, Cratylus mystifies me; he says that there is a fitness of names, but he never explains what is this fitness, so that I cannot tell whether his obscurity is intended or not. Tell me now, Cratylus, here in the presence of Socrates, do you agree in what Socrates has been saying about names, or have you something better of your own? and if you have, tell me what your view is, and then you will either learn of Socrates, or Socrates and I will learn of you.

CRATYLUS
Well, but surely, Hermogenes, you do not suppose that you can learn, or I explain, any subject of importance all in a moment; at any rate, not such a subject as language, which is, perhaps, the very greatest of all.

HERMOGENES
No, indeed; but, as Hesiod says, and I agree with him, 'to add little to little' is worth while. And, therefore, if you think that you can add anything at all, however small, to our knowledge, take a little trouble and oblige Socrates, and me too, who certainly have a claim upon you.

SOCRATES
I am by no means positive, Cratylus, in the view which Hermogenes and myself have worked out; and therefore do not hesitate to say what you think, which if it be better than my own view I shall gladly

accept. And I should not be at all surprized to find that you have found some better notion. For you have evidently reflected on these matters and have had teachers, and if you have really a better theory of the truth of names, you may count me in the number of your disciples.

CRATYLUS
You are right, Socrates, in saying that I have made a study of these matters, and I might possibly convert you into a disciple. But I fear that the opposite is more probable, and I already find myself moved to say to you what Achilles in the 'Prayers' says to Ajax,--

'Illustrious Ajax, son of Telamon, lord of the people, You appear to have spoken in all things much to my mind.'

And you, Socrates, appear to me to be an oracle, and to give answers much to my mind, whether you are inspired by Euthyphro, or whether some Muse may have long been an inhabitant of your breast, unconsciously to yourself.

SOCRATES
Excellent Cratylus, I have long been wondering at my own wisdom; I cannot trust myself. And I think that I ought to stop and ask myself What am I saying? for there is nothing worse than self-deception--when the deceiver is always at home and always with you--it is quite terrible, and therefore I ought often to retrace my steps and endeavour to 'look fore and aft,' in the words of the aforesaid Homer. And now let me see; where are we? Have we not been saying that the correct name indicates the nature of the thing:--has this proposition been sufficiently proven?

CRATYLUS
Yes, Socrates, what you say, as I am disposed to think, is quite true.

SOCRATES
Names, then, are given in order to instruct?

CRATYLUS
Certainly.

SOCRATES
And naming is an art, and has artificers?

CRATYLUS
Yes.

SOCRATES
And who are they?

CRATYLUS
The legislators, of whom you spoke at first.

SOCRATES
And does this art grow up among men like other arts? Let me explain what I mean: of painters, some are better and some worse?

CRATYLUS

Yes.

SOCRATES

The better painters execute their works, I mean their figures, better, and the worse execute them worse; and of builders also, the better sort build fairer houses, and the worse build them worse.

CRATYLUS

True.

SOCRATES

And among legislators, there are some who do their work better and some worse?

CRATYLUS

No; there I do not agree with you.

SOCRATES

Then you do not think that some laws are better and others worse?

CRATYLUS

No, indeed.

SOCRATES

Or that one name is better than another?

CRATYLUS

Certainly not.

SOCRATES

Then all names are rightly imposed?

CRATYLUS

Yes, if they are names at all.

SOCRATES

Well, what do you say to the name of our friend Hermogenes, which was mentioned before:--assuming that he has nothing of the nature of Hermes in him, shall we say that this is a wrong name, or not his name at all?

CRATYLUS

I should reply that Hermogenes is not his name at all, but only appears to be his, and is really the name of somebody else, who has the nature which corresponds to it.

SOCRATES

And if a man were to call him Hermogenes, would he not be even speaking falsely? For there may be a doubt whether you can call him Hermogenes, if he is not.

CRATYLUS
What do you mean?

SOCRATES
Are you maintaining that falsehood is impossible? For if this is your meaning I should answer, that there have been plenty of liars in all ages.

CRATYLUS
Why, Socrates, how can a man say that which is not?--say something and yet say nothing? For is not falsehood saying the thing which is not?

SOCRATES
Your argument, friend, is too subtle for a man of my age. But I should like to know whether you are one of those philosophers who think that falsehood may be spoken but not said?

CRATYLUS
Neither spoken nor said.

SOCRATES
Nor uttered nor addressed? For example: If a person, saluting you in a foreign country, were to take your hand and say: 'Hail, Athenian stranger, Hermogenes, son of Smicrion'--these words, whether spoken, said, uttered, or addressed, would have no application to you but only to our friend Hermogenes, or perhaps to nobody at all?

CRATYLUS
In my opinion, Socrates, the speaker would only be talking nonsense.

SOCRATES
Well, but that will be quite enough for me, if you will tell me whether the nonsense would be true or false, or partly true and partly false:--which is all that I want to know.

CRATYLUS
I should say that he would be putting himself in motion to no purpose; and that his words would be an unmeaning sound like the noise of hammering at a brazen pot.

SOCRATES
But let us see, Cratylus, whether we cannot find a meeting-point, for you would admit that the name is not the same with the thing named?

CRATYLUS
I should.

SOCRATES
And would you further acknowledge that the name is an imitation of the thing?

CRATYLUS
Certainly.

SOCRATES

And you would say that pictures are also imitations of things, but in another way?

CRATYLUS

Yes.

SOCRATES

I believe you may be right, but I do not rightly understand you. Please to say, then, whether both sorts of imitation (I mean both pictures or words) are not equally attributable and applicable to the things of which they are the imitation.

CRATYLUS

They are.

SOCRATES

First look at the matter thus: you may attribute the likeness of the man to the man, and of the woman to the woman; and so on?

CRATYLUS

Certainly.

SOCRATES

And conversely you may attribute the likeness of the man to the woman, and of the woman to the man?

CRATYLUS

Very true.

SOCRATES

And are both modes of assigning them right, or only the first?

CRATYLUS

Only the first.

SOCRATES

That is to say, the mode of assignment which attributes to each that which belongs to them and is like them?

CRATYLUS

That is my view.

SOCRATES

Now then, as I am desirous that we being friends should have a good understanding about the argument, let me state my view to you: the first mode of assignment, whether applied to figures or to names, I call right, and when applied to names only, true as well as right; and the other mode of giving and assigning the name which is unlike, I call wrong, and in the case of names, false as well as wrong.

CRATYLUS

That may be true, Socrates, in the case of pictures; they may be wrongly assigned; but not in the case of names--they must be always right.

SOCRATES
Why, what is the difference? May I not go to a man and say to him, 'This is your picture,' showing him his own likeness, or perhaps the likeness of a woman; and when I say 'show,' I mean bring before the sense of sight.

CRATYLUS
Certainly.

SOCRATES
And may I not go to him again, and say, 'This is your name'?--for the name, like the picture, is an imitation. May I not say to him--'This is your name'? and may I not then bring to his sense of hearing the imitation of himself, when I say, 'This is a man'; or of a female of the human species, when I say, 'This is a woman,' as the case may be? Is not all that quite possible?

CRATYLUS
I would fain agree with you, Socrates; and therefore I say, Granted.

SOCRATES
That is very good of you, if I am right, which need hardly be disputed at present. But if I can assign names as well as pictures to objects, the right assignment of them we may call truth, and the wrong assignment of them falsehood. Now if there be such a wrong assignment of names, there may also be a wrong or inappropriate assignment of verbs; and if of names and verbs then of the sentences, which are made up of them. What do you say, Cratylus?

CRATYLUS
I agree; and think that what you say is very true.

SOCRATES
And further, primitive nouns may be compared to pictures, and in pictures you may either give all the appropriate colours and figures, or you may not give them all--some may be wanting; or there may be too many or too much of them--may there not?

CRATYLUS
Very true.

SOCRATES
And he who gives all gives a perfect picture or figure; and he who takes away or adds also gives a picture or figure, but not a good one.

CRATYLUS
Yes.

SOCRATES
In like manner, he who by syllables and letters imitates the nature of things, if he gives all that is appropriate will produce a good image, or in other words a name; but if he subtracts or perhaps adds a

little, he will make an image but not a good one; whence I infer that some names are well and others ill made.

CRATYLUS
That is true.

SOCRATES
Then the artist of names may be sometimes good, or he may be bad?

CRATYLUS
Yes.

SOCRATES
And this artist of names is called the legislator?

CRATYLUS
Yes.

SOCRATES
Then like other artists the legislator may be good or he may be bad; it must surely be so if our former admissions hold good?

CRATYLUS
Very true, Socrates; but the case of language, you see, is different; for when by the help of grammar we assign the letters alpha or beta, or any other letters to a certain name, then, if we add, or subtract, or misplace a letter, the name which is written is not only written wrongly, but not written at all; and in any of these cases becomes other than a name.

SOCRATES
But I doubt whether your view is altogether correct, Cratylus.

CRATYLUS
How so?

SOCRATES
I believe that what you say may be true about numbers, which must be just what they are, or not be at all; for example, the number ten at once becomes other than ten if a unit be added or subtracted, and so of any other number: but this does not apply to that which is qualitative or to anything which is represented under an image. I should say rather that the image, if expressing in every point the entire reality, would no longer be an image. Let us suppose the existence of two objects: one of them shall be Cratylus, and the other the image of Cratylus; and we will suppose, further, that some God makes not only a representation such as a painter would make of your outward form and colour, but also creates an inward organization like yours, having the same warmth and softness; and into this infuses motion, and soul, and mind, such as you have, and in a word copies all your qualities, and places them by you in another form; would you say that this was Cratylus and the image of Cratylus, or that there were two Cratyluses?

CRATYLUS

I should say that there were two Cratyluses.

SOCRATES
Then you see, my friend, that we must find some other principle of truth in images, and also in names; and not insist that an image is no longer an image when something is added or subtracted. Do you not perceive that images are very far from having qualities which are the exact counterpart of the realities which they represent?

CRATYLUS
Yes, I see.

SOCRATES
But then how ridiculous would be the effect of names on things, if they were exactly the same with them! For they would be the doubles of them, and no one would be able to determine which were the names and which were the realities.

CRATYLUS
Quite true.

SOCRATES
Then fear not, but have the courage to admit that one name may be correctly and another incorrectly given; and do not insist that the name shall be exactly the same with the thing; but allow the occasional substitution of a wrong letter, and if of a letter also of a noun in a sentence, and if of a noun in a sentence also of a sentence which is not appropriate to the matter, and acknowledge that the thing may be named, and described, so long as the general character of the thing which you are describing is retained; and this, as you will remember, was remarked by Hermogenes and myself in the particular instance of the names of the letters.

CRATYLUS
Yes, I remember.

SOCRATES
Good; and when the general character is preserved, even if some of the proper letters are wanting, still the thing is signified;--well, if all the letters are given; not well, when only a few of them are given. I think that we had better admit this, lest we be punished like travellers in Aegina who wander about the street late at night: and be likewise told by truth herself that we have arrived too late; or if not, you must find out some new notion of correctness of names, and no longer maintain that a name is the expression of a thing in letters or syllables; for if you say both, you will be inconsistent with yourself.

CRATYLUS
I quite acknowledge, Socrates, what you say to be very reasonable.

SOCRATES
Then as we are agreed thus far, let us ask ourselves whether a name rightly imposed ought not to have the proper letters.

CRATYLUS
Yes.

SOCRATES

And the proper letters are those which are like the things?

CRATYLUS

Yes.

SOCRATES

Enough then of names which are rightly given. And in names which are incorrectly given, the greater part may be supposed to be made up of proper and similar letters, or there would be no likeness; but there will be likewise a part which is improper and spoils the beauty and formation of the word: you would admit that?

CRATYLUS

There would be no use, Socrates, in my quarrelling with you, since I cannot be satisfied that a name which is incorrectly given is a name at all.

SOCRATES

Do you admit a name to be the representation of a thing?

CRATYLUS

Yes, I do.

SOCRATES

But do you not allow that some nouns are primitive, and some derived?

CRATYLUS

Yes, I do.

SOCRATES

Then if you admit that primitive or first nouns are representations of things, is there any better way of framing representations than by assimilating them to the objects as much as you can; or do you prefer the notion of Hermogenes and of many others, who say that names are conventional, and have a meaning to those who have agreed about them, and who have previous knowledge of the things intended by them, and that convention is the only principle; and whether you abide by our present convention, or make a new and opposite one, according to which you call small great and great small-- that, they would say, makes no difference, if you are only agreed. Which of these two notions do you prefer?

CRATYLUS

Representation by likeness, Socrates, is infinitely better than representation by any chance sign.

SOCRATES

Very good: but if the name is to be like the thing, the letters out of which the first names are composed must also be like things. Returning to the image of the picture, I would ask, How could any one ever compose a picture which would be like anything at all, if there were not pigments in nature which resembled the things imitated, and out of which the picture is composed?

CRATYLUS

Impossible.

SOCRATES

No more could names ever resemble any actually existing thing, unless the original elements of which they are compounded bore some degree of resemblance to the objects of which the names are the imitation: And the original elements are letters?

CRATYLUS

Yes.

SOCRATES

Let me now invite you to consider what Hermogenes and I were saying about sounds. Do you agree with me that the letter rho is expressive of rapidity, motion, and hardness? Were we right or wrong in saying so?

CRATYLUS

I should say that you were right.

SOCRATES

And that lamda was expressive of smoothness, and softness, and the like?

CRATYLUS

There again you were right.

SOCRATES

And yet, as you are aware, that which is called by us sklerotes, is by the Eretrians called skleroter.

CRATYLUS

Very true.

SOCRATES

But are the letters rho and sigma equivalents; and is there the same significance to them in the termination rho, which there is to us in sigma, or is there no significance to one of us?

CRATYLUS

Nay, surely there is a significance to both of us.

SOCRATES

In as far as they are like, or in as far as they are unlike?

CRATYLUS

In as far as they are like.

SOCRATES

Are they altogether alike?

CRATYLUS

Yes; for the purpose of expressing motion.

SOCRATES
And what do you say of the insertion of the lamda? for that is expressive not of hardness but of softness.

CRATYLUS
Why, perhaps the letter lamda is wrongly inserted, Socrates, and should be altered into rho, as you were saying to Hermogenes and in my opinion rightly, when you spoke of adding and subtracting letters upon occasion.

SOCRATES
Good. But still the word is intelligible to both of us; when I say skleros (hard), you know what I mean.

CRATYLUS
Yes, my dear friend, and the explanation of that is custom.

SOCRATES
And what is custom but convention? I utter a sound which I understand, and you know that I understand the meaning of the sound: this is what you are saying?

CRATYLUS
Yes.

SOCRATES
And if when I speak you know my meaning, there is an indication given by me to you?

CRATYLUS
Yes.

SOCRATES
This indication of my meaning may proceed from unlike as well as from like, for example in the lamda of sklerotes. But if this is true, then you have made a convention with yourself, and the correctness of a name turns out to be convention, since letters which are unlike are indicative equally with those which are like, if they are sanctioned by custom and convention. And even supposing that you distinguish custom from convention ever so much, still you must say that the signification of words is given by custom and not by likeness, for custom may indicate by the unlike as well as by the like. But as we are agreed thus far, Cratylus (for I shall assume that your silence gives consent), then custom and convention must be supposed to contribute to the indication of our thoughts; for suppose we take the instance of number, how can you ever imagine, my good friend, that you will find names resembling every individual number, unless you allow that which you term convention and agreement to have authority in determining the correctness of names? I quite agree with you that words should as far as possible resemble things; but I fear that this dragging in of resemblance, as Hermogenes says, is a shabby thing, which has to be supplemented by the mechanical aid of convention with a view to correctness; for I believe that if we could always, or almost always, use likenesses, which are perfectly appropriate, this would be the most perfect state of language; as the opposite is the most imperfect. But let me ask you, what is the force of names, and what is the use of them?

CRATYLUS

The use of names, Socrates, as I should imagine, is to inform: the simple truth is, that he who knows names knows also the things which are expressed by them.

SOCRATES
I suppose you mean to say, Cratylus, that as the name is, so also is the thing; and that he who knows the one will also know the other, because they are similars, and all similars fall under the same art or science; and therefore you would say that he who knows names will also know things.

CRATYLUS
That is precisely what I mean.

SOCRATES
But let us consider what is the nature of this information about things which, according to you, is given us by names. Is it the best sort of information? or is there any other? What do you say?

CRATYLUS
I believe that to be both the only and the best sort of information about them; there can be no other.

SOCRATES
But do you believe that in the discovery of them, he who discovers the names discovers also the things; or is this only the method of instruction, and is there some other method of enquiry and discovery.

CRATYLUS
I certainly believe that the methods of enquiry and discovery are of the same nature as instruction.

SOCRATES
Well, but do you not see, Cratylus, that he who follows names in the search after things, and analyses their meaning, is in great danger of being deceived?

CRATYLUS
How so?

SOCRATES
Why clearly he who first gave names gave them according to his conception of the things which they signified--did he not?

CRATYLUS
True.

SOCRATES
And if his conception was erroneous, and he gave names according to his conception, in what position shall we who are his followers find ourselves? Shall we not be deceived by him?

CRATYLUS
But, Socrates, am I not right in thinking that he must surely have known; or else, as I was saying, his names would not be names at all? And you have a clear proof that he has not missed the truth, and the proof is--that he is perfectly consistent. Did you ever observe in speaking that all the words which you utter have a common character and purpose?

SOCRATES

But that, friend Cratylus, is no answer. For if he did begin in error, he may have forced the remainder into agreement with the original error and with himself; there would be nothing strange in this, any more than in geometrical diagrams, which have often a slight and invisible flaw in the first part of the process, and are consistently mistaken in the long deductions which follow. And this is the reason why every man should expend his chief thought and attention on the consideration of his first principles:-- are they or are they not rightly laid down? and when he has duly sifted them, all the rest will follow. Now I should be astonished to find that names are really consistent. And here let us revert to our former discussion: Were we not saying that all things are in motion and progress and flux, and that this idea of motion is expressed by names? Do you not conceive that to be the meaning of them?

CRATYLUS

Yes; that is assuredly their meaning, and the true meaning.

SOCRATES

Let us revert to episteme (knowledge) and observe how ambiguous this word is, seeming rather to signify stopping the soul at things than going round with them; and therefore we should leave the beginning as at present, and not reject the epsilon, but make an insertion of an iota instead of an epsilon (not pioteme, but epiisteme). Take another example: bebaion (sure) is clearly the expression of station and position, and not of motion. Again, the word istoria (enquiry) bears upon the face of it the stopping (istanai) of the stream; and the word piston (faithful) certainly indicates cessation of motion; then, again, mneme (memory), as any one may see, expresses rest in the soul, and not motion. Moreover, words such as amartia and sumphora, which have a bad sense, viewed in the light of their etymologies will be the same as sunesis and episteme and other words which have a good sense (compare omartein, sunienai, epesthai, sumpheresthai); and much the same may be said of amathia and akolasia, for amathia may be explained as e ama theo iontos poreia, and akolasia as e akolouthia tois pragmasin. Thus the names which in these instances we find to have the worst sense, will turn out to be framed on the same principle as those which have the best. And any one I believe who would take the trouble might find many other examples in which the giver of names indicates, not that things are in motion or progress, but that they are at rest; which is the opposite of motion.

CRATYLUS

Yes, Socrates, but observe; the greater number express motion.

SOCRATES

What of that, Cratylus? Are we to count them like votes? and is correctness of names the voice of the majority? Are we to say of whichever sort there are most, those are the true ones?

CRATYLUS

No; that is not reasonable.

SOCRATES

Certainly not. But let us have done with this question and proceed to another, about which I should like to know whether you think with me. Were we not lately acknowledging that the first givers of names in states, both Hellenic and barbarous, were the legislators, and that the art which gave names was the art of the legislator?

CRATYLUS

Quite true.

SOCRATES

Tell me, then, did the first legislators, who were the givers of the first names, know or not know the things which they named?

CRATYLUS

They must have known, Socrates.

SOCRATES

Why, yes, friend Cratylus, they could hardly have been ignorant.

CRATYLUS

I should say not.

SOCRATES

Let us return to the point from which we digressed. You were saying, if you remember, that he who gave names must have known the things which he named; are you still of that opinion?

CRATYLUS

I am.

SOCRATES

And would you say that the giver of the first names had also a knowledge of the things which he named?

CRATYLUS

I should.

SOCRATES

But how could he have learned or discovered things from names if the primitive names were not yet given? For, if we are correct in our view, the only way of learning and discovering things, is either to discover names for ourselves or to learn them from others.

CRATYLUS

I think that there is a good deal in what you say, Socrates.

SOCRATES

But if things are only to be known through names, how can we suppose that the givers of names had knowledge, or were legislators before there were names at all, and therefore before they could have known them?

CRATYLUS

I believe, Socrates, the true account of the matter to be, that a power more than human gave things their first names, and that the names which are thus given are necessarily their true names.

SOCRATES

Then how came the giver of the names, if he was an inspired being or God, to contradict himself? For were we not saying just now that he made some names expressive of rest and others of motion? Were we mistaken?

CRATYLUS
But I suppose one of the two not to be names at all.

SOCRATES
And which, then, did he make, my good friend; those which are expressive of rest, or those which are expressive of motion? This is a point which, as I said before, cannot be determined by counting them.

CRATYLUS
No; not in that way, Socrates.

SOCRATES
But if this is a battle of names, some of them asserting that they are like the truth, others contending that THEY are, how or by what criterion are we to decide between them? For there are no other names to which appeal can be made, but obviously recourse must be had to another standard which, without employing names, will make clear which of the two are right; and this must be a standard which shows the truth of things.

CRATYLUS
I agree.

SOCRATES
But if that is true, Cratylus, then I suppose that things may be known without names?

CRATYLUS
Clearly.

SOCRATES
But how would you expect to know them? What other way can there be of knowing them, except the true and natural way, through their affinities, when they are akin to each other, and through themselves? For that which is other and different from them must signify something other and different from them.

CRATYLUS
What you are saying is, I think, true.

SOCRATES
Well, but reflect; have we not several times acknowledged that names rightly given are the likenesses and images of the things which they name?

CRATYLUS
Yes.

SOCRATES

Let us suppose that to any extent you please you can learn things through the medium of names, and suppose also that you can learn them from the things themselves--which is likely to be the nobler and clearer way; to learn of the image, whether the image and the truth of which the image is the expression have been rightly conceived, or to learn of the truth whether the truth and the image of it have been duly executed?

CRATYLUS
I should say that we must learn of the truth.

SOCRATES
How real existence is to be studied or discovered is, I suspect, beyond you and me. But we may admit so much, that the knowledge of things is not to be derived from names. No; they must be studied and investigated in themselves.

CRATYLUS
Clearly, Socrates.

SOCRATES
There is another point. I should not like us to be imposed upon by the appearance of such a multitude of names, all tending in the same direction. I myself do not deny that the givers of names did really give them under the idea that all things were in motion and flux; which was their sincere but, I think, mistaken opinion. And having fallen into a kind of whirlpool themselves, they are carried round, and want to drag us in after them. There is a matter, master Cratylus, about which I often dream, and should like to ask your opinion: Tell me, whether there is or is not any absolute beauty or good, or any other absolute existence?

CRATYLUS
Certainly, Socrates, I think so.

SOCRATES
Then let us seek the true beauty: not asking whether a face is fair, or anything of that sort, for all such things appear to be in a flux; but let us ask whether the true beauty is not always beautiful.

CRATYLUS
Certainly.

SOCRATES
And can we rightly speak of a beauty which is always passing away, and is first this and then that; must not the same thing be born and retire and vanish while the word is in our mouths?

CRATYLUS
Undoubtedly.

SOCRATES
Then how can that be a real thing which is never in the same state? for obviously things which are the same cannot change while they remain the same; and if they are always the same and in the same state, and never depart from their original form, they can never change or be moved.

CRATYLUS

Certainly they cannot.

SOCRATES

Nor yet can they be known by any one; for at the moment that the observer approaches, then they become other and of another nature, so that you cannot get any further in knowing their nature or state, for you cannot know that which has no state.

CRATYLUS

True.

SOCRATES

Nor can we reasonably say, Cratylus, that there is knowledge at all, if everything is in a state of transition and there is nothing abiding; for knowledge too cannot continue to be knowledge unless continuing always to abide and exist. But if the very nature of knowledge changes, at the time when the change occurs there will be no knowledge; and if the transition is always going on, there will always be no knowledge, and, according to this view, there will be no one to know and nothing to be known: but if that which knows and that which is known exists ever, and the beautiful and the good and every other thing also exist, then I do not think that they can resemble a process or flux, as we were just now supposing. Whether there is this eternal nature in things, or whether the truth is what Heracleitus and his followers and many others say, is a question hard to determine; and no man of sense will like to put himself or the education of his mind in the power of names: neither will he so far trust names or the givers of names as to be confident in any knowledge which condemns himself and other existences to an unhealthy state of unreality; he will not believe that all things leak like a pot, or imagine that the world is a man who has a running at the nose. This may be true, Cratylus, but is also very likely to be untrue; and therefore I would not have you be too easily persuaded of it. Reflect well and like a man, and do not easily accept such a doctrine; for you are young and of an age to learn. And when you have found the truth, come and tell me.

CRATYLUS

I will do as you say, though I can assure you, Socrates, that I have been considering the matter already, and the result of a great deal of trouble and consideration is that I incline to Heracleitus.

SOCRATES

Then, another day, my friend, when you come back, you shall give me a lesson; but at present, go into the country, as you are intending, and Hermogenes shall set you on your way.

CRATYLUS

Very good, Socrates; I hope, however, that you will continue to think about these things yourself.

www.ingramcontent.com/pod-product-compliance
Lightning Source LLC
Chambersburg PA
CBHW060122050426
42448CB00010B/1990